Portland's

Rose City Ghosts I

By Jefferson Davis

Published by Norsemen Ventures L. L. C.
Copyright © 2007 by Jefferson Davis
Printed by Central Plains Book, KS

The following stories have appeared in earlier Jefferson Davis books, © 1997 – 2001: The Crystal Ballroom, The Benson Hotel, The Heathman Hotel, The Noisy Ghosts of Piggot's Castle, KWJJ is on the Air, and Pittock Mansion

Some elements of stories from the following stories have appeared in other Jefferson Davis works: Old Town Pizza, Dan and Louis Oyster Bar, Kell's Irish Pub, The White Eagle Saloon, © 1997 – 2001:

Davis, Jefferson Dale
        Portland's Rose City Ghosts I
                1. Ghosts and Paranormal
                2. Spirituality and folklore
                3. Portland, Oregon History
                4. Includes Index

Library of Congress Control Number: 2008901642
ISBN: 978-1893186-11-8

Acknowledgements

Like all of my books, this one would not have been possible without the help of a lot of people. It is a toss up between David Schargal and my clairvoyant friend Karan as to who motivated me the most to write this book. David for wanting me to help him with his tour, including training his guides, and to Karan for walking around lots of places, sometimes with a headache. A lot of time with a headache.

Of course, I want to thank the business owners and employers who sat down to talk about their experiences, despite fear of ridicule. You gave this book the flavor of your real live experiences. Thank you Lisa Schroeder of Mama Mia's, Ed Lawrence of the Crystal Ballroom, Chuck Hughes and everyone else at the White Eagle Saloon, Mariane M., and Brian from the Hotel Vintage Plaza, Tom Carrollo of the U.S. Bank building, the Wachsmuth family at Dan and Louis, Randy for his experiences at the Carabou Club and Cobalt Lounge, Mike at Hoodoo Antiques, Adam at Old Town Pizza, as well as Fran, for her experiences there. And for sending me emails, thanks to Amy, Joe.

Thanks to the tour guides at Portland Walking Tours for listening to me rattle on about ghosts and history. Thanks to my wife Janine and friend Lili St Crowe for reading this manuscript. And thanks to you for buying and reading it.

Be safe out there,
Jeff Davis

Table of Contents

Introduction

Welcome to *Rose City Ghosts, Volume I,* an outgrowth of some old and very new work. In 2007, David Schargel from Portland Walking Tours contacted me and asked my help in setting up a spooky walk of downtown Portland. I was flattered, interested, and a bit alarmed. I believe that city ghost walks are a good way to educate people about the history of a city as well as scaring tourists. At the same time, I was busy writing *Weird Washington,* so I wrote very, very fast.

David and I discussed what I knew about haunted Portland, including places like the Pittock Mansion, Powell's Books, and the Crystal Ballroom. Most of these were outside the area that David was interested in. He was interested in a few places, like the White Eagle Saloon, and Kell's Irish Pub. However, David wanted updated information. So, with the help of my trusty clairvoyant friend Karan, I went back to downtown Portland and gathered many new stories for his tour; *Portland, Beyond Bizarre.*

I hate buying a new book by an author I like, only to find that it reuses past stories. Guilty. I went through my previous works, and collected some stories for this book. I did this because it would not have made sense to publish a book on Portland's ghosts without mentioning these haunts. I edited and revised stories on Piggot's Castle, the old KWJJ radio station, Pittock Mansion, the Crystal Ballroom, the Benson Hotel, and the Heathman Hotel. I referenced earlier stories on Mama Mia's, Kell's Irish Pub, Dan and Louis Oyster Bar, adding more details.

I promise you that most of the stories you will read in this book are new, or (as in the case of the White Eagle,) I have some new and interesting accounts of an old and popular haunt. I intend to write at least three books on haunted locations within the City of Portland. Since Portland is the largest city in Oregon, a single volume of collected stories would make a book of at least 300 pages. Putting one volume this size together would have taken me three years. So I decided to split the work up and put out several books over the next few years. This volume includes haunts in the oldest portions of Portland, around the west bank of the Willamette River. This includes downtown Portland as well as other well known haunts like the Pittock Mansion, and a few others.

I divided this book geographically, using Burnside as the primary marker. Readers will notice that downtown locations are listed first south and east from Burnside. Then I started from Burnside again, and listed locations heading north. Welcome.

Founding Portland and its Ghosts

Portland is not the oldest United States settlement on the Willamette River. U.S. settlers, led by John McLoughlin settled in Oregon City, at the Willamette Falls. Although ships touched down on the banks of the Willamette River,

between Oregon City and Fort Vancouver, they did not stay long. Most continued toward Oregon City, but many of the larger ships could not make it because of hidden rocks. Instead, they and later settlers looked for a place with a deeper anchorage for a new city. They found it on what may have been an abandoned Native American settlement.

Before the arrival of Europeans in the Pacific Northwest, a series of European and Asian diseases swept across North America. Perhaps the first plague to arrive in the Northwest was smallpox, in the late 1700s. It could have come from trading vessels on the coast, or it could have spread overland from as far away as Florida or Mexico. These plagues continued through the 1800s. These were probably different diseases, but each time they struck, 80% to 90% of the native people died.

In 1829, the *Owyhee* sailed up the Willamette, and anchored below the Clackamas Rapids. After they sailed away, ninety percent of the Clackamas living there died from a plague of some kind. In the later 1830s, the Chinookan peoples of the lower Columbia and the Callapuyan people of the Willamette Rivers suffered from what historians called, "intermittent fever," which might have been malaria. By the census of 1850, only 88 Clackamas, and a few hundred Callapuya lived in the Willamette Valley, where before there had been thousands.

The surviving native people often abandoned their settlements, and everyone was afraid to enter afterward. In some cases, some brave soul entered the villages and burned them to the ground. Over time, even the unburned villages tumbled down, and people forgot they ever existed. So whether by plague or other factors, by the 1840s, much of the west bank of the Columbia River was abandoned by Native Americans, as their settlements vanished into wilderness.

There are many stories about how Messers. Overton, Pettygrove, and Lovejoy selected and laid out the site of Portland, Oregon. Most agree that in November 1843, Overton and Lovejoy were traveling from Oregon City to Vancouver by canoe, and stopped where they thought they could found a new town. The channel was deep enough for large ships to anchor safely, and they were attracted to the site by a lack of massive trees along the riverbank.

There was very little underbrush along the riverbank from present day Washington to Jefferson Streets. Both men believed that the area had been cleared by Native Americans, as a temporary campsite. It may have even been an abandoned village. While the Pioneers needed trees for lumber and firewood, old growth trees took a lot of work to cut down; and the stumps were a nuisance. As Portland grew, it became known as Stumptown.

Overton sold half his land claim to Asa Lovejoy for a quarter of a dollar! Later Pettygrove bought the other half, before Overton disappeared into history. Pettygrove and Lovejoy surveyed out a town site in the summer of 1844, then built a log house and sawmill near the place where Washington Street meets the Willamette River. They flipped a coin, agreeing to name their new town after the winner's home town. Pettygrove was from Portland, Maine, while Lovejoy was from Boston, Massachusetts; guess who won.

Truth and Legends of Portland's Shanghai tunnels

Within a few years, Portland became the major port of the Lower Columbia River, where tall ships docked to take on commodities like preserved salmon, wheat, and lumber, among other things. In these early days, the rains made Portland's streets muddy and treacherous for stevedores loading and unloading many of these ships. Rather than paving the streets, merchants protected their goods by tunneling westward, into the hillsides above the docks.

These tunnels were originally only a few blocks long, paralleling the streets, with several entrances into the basements of various businesses. Soon side tunnels running north and south linked to the original tunnels. Eventually city engineers covered the dirt or brick tunnel ceilings with concrete sidewalks. To give light into these tunnels, the sidewalks have several glass panes embedded in them. Over time, ultraviolet sunlight has turned these *light wells* blue, indicating they are over 100 years old.

While these tunnels were used for commerce during the day, some served less-legal purposes at night. As a thriving port, Portland always had a number of sailors who did not want to ship out again after arriving. Ships also arrived short-handed after long trips, and needed some new sailors. While the ship captains advertised for new sailors, not enough signed up for long voyages to places like Shanghai. Many saloon owners and others, kidnapped sailors or other able-bodied men, and received a "finder's" when they delivered their captives to the ship captain. Someone who was kidnapped was "Shanghaied," and the person who kidnapped them was a "Shanghaier," or a "Crimp."

Surprisingly, elements of Shanghaiing were legal. In 1790, the United States passed a Federal law where any sailor who signed up to work on a vessel would go to prison, if they deserted before the end of the voyage. The crimp was an essential player in locking sailors into this law. At that time, sailors received a bonus when they signed up for a voyage. This paid for any equipment they needed for the trip. The crimp acted as the agent for the unconscious man, forging the shanghaied man's signature for the advance. They also provided the "sailor" an equipment bag the cost of which was deducted from the sailor's signing bonus, at a thoroughly inflated price. When the men awoke, they found themselves several hours out to sea, and indebted to the ship's captain.

Portland had many infamous places where sailors and lumberjacks always went with friends. Some of Portland's saloons had trapdoors, where a man might fall through into the basement if he had too much to drink. If he was still on his feet, it was not for long, because there was usually a bully boy with a club waiting for him. Some Crimps operated boarding houses, and waited for their victims to come to

them. Among them were places like Erickson's Saloon.

In the 1880s, many states cracked down on crimping, and passed laws eliminating the sign up bonus. There were loopholes in the law, and crimps continued operating. In 1915, Congress passed the Seaman's Act, which made crimping a federal crime. At the same time, sailing ships gave way to steam powered vessels, which needed only half the crew, creating a surplus of able-bodied seamen. When combined with the new anti-crimping laws, Shanghaiing proved both unprofitable and not worth the risk to try.

Shanghaiers did not use all of Portland's tunnels. Many of Portland's early buildings were heated using steam, which was piped from building to building through tunnels. Electricity, gas and other utilities also travelled underground. In some cases, these upgrades used the older tunnels, but most of the time, engineers built new tunnels. Over time, many of the disused tunnels connecting Portland's waterfront were abandoned, and many businesses also bricked up the entrances in their basements. In the 1990s, the City of Portland finished the job for them.

Some business owners have found cells where prisoners were stashed, waiting to be loaded onto waiting ships. Some of them certainly perished during that wait. Some of Portland's basement tunnels have been improved, for customer use, like the cigar bar at Kell's Irish Pub. So if you go into the basement of any waterfront business, listen for the ghosts telling you the sad tale of their last drink.

The early Pioneers and the Oregon Trail

In 1843, there were only 700 settlers in the Oregon Country, which included what is now Oregon, Washington, and part of Idaho. In the early 1840s, many of the settlers gathered and held a series of meetings, and set up their own government. They lobbied the United States Congress to recognize them as an American Territory. By 1845, there were 3,000 settlers. In 1848, Congress created the Oregon Territory, and began the process of opening up lands west of the Cascade Mountains. Initially the first Settlers took land claims of 640 acres of land, which is one square mile.

In 1850, Congress passed the Donation Land Act, which recognized earlier claims, and set up grants for new settlers of 320 acres of land per man, with more for wives, and children. All they had to do was build a home, "improve" the land and live there a certain number of years. While I say, 'All they had to do…' It was quite a struggle, cutting down trees, planting crops, and surviving.

In 1855, the government created the Grand Ronde Indian Reservation, and removed most of the surviving Native Americans from the Willamette River. That same year, thirty thousand emigrants settled west of the Cascades. The only way to get there was by sea, or overland by wagon, on the more popular Oregon Trail. Another 600,000 Pioneers traveled the Oregon Trail in the following years.

The Oregon Trail saw most of its travelers between 1850 and 1869. In 1869, the first transcontinental railroad opened up, and most emigrants preferred traveling a couple of weeks on a train to spending six months crossing North America by wagon. Not all of the people who took the Oregon Trail settled in the Willamette Valley. Along the way, there were several branching routes which led to Southern Oregon, or California.

At least 650,000 people traveled the Oregon Trail in those years. This may not sound like many people, but it was a huge percentage of the American population. The U.S. Census of 1850 recorded all household members, including women, children and slaves. It totaled over 23 million people. In 1860, there were nearly 31.5 million people, an increase of 35 percent. In 1870, United States' population was about 38.5 million. So during the high point in the Oregon Trail, those 650,000 people meant more than 15% of all Americans went west in search of a better future.

Perhaps ten percent of the people (65,000) who traveled the Oregon Trail died along the way, which was nine

Pioneer Woman's Grave   Courtesy US Forest Service

deaths for every mile. (That is over 1% of all Americans.) Some of them died in accidents, from starvation, etc., but many died of diseases, like cholera. In 1840, a cholera pandemic began in India, and spread worldwide. It reached the United States in the mid 1840s, and peaked in 1850, but lingered in places like the Oregon Trail for many more years.

Cholera outbreaks are usually caused by a contaminated water supply. People can carry the disease for several days without realizing it. However, once the symptoms set in, the disease acts quickly. An infected person might feel fine in the morning, but by noon, they could develop an intense stomachache. A few minutes after that, the victim would develop continuous diarrhea, and probably convulsive vomiting. People do not die from cholera itself, they die from the symptoms of dehydration.

The dehydration from the diarrhea is so intense, that within hours, the victim's skin wrinkles and turn blue, as their bodies literally dry out. At that time, if the cholera did not kill the victim within the first day, they usually recovered. Unfortunately, only about half of them survived. The survivors and dead both spread the disease in the form of human waste and garbage. A wagon train suffering from cholera might stop at a waterhole and contaminate the water. For weeks, Native American and Pioneer alike would become infected, and spread the disease. At that time, the treatment for cholera was fairly simple, constant replenishment of the patient's water. Unfortunately, there was not always enough fresh water, or people could not keep it down.

Searching for forgotten graveyards

Tradition says at least one Native American or Pioneer graveyard was near the spot where Lovejoy and Pettygrove settled. No one seems certain where it is. Oral traditions (or urban legends) mention a cholera epidemic linked to the Skidmore fountains, leading to mass burials. Another legend talks about human bones found in the basement of one of Portland's nearby historic homes.

My clairvoyant friend Karan and I walked around Portland, to places where rumors suggested there was a graveyard. Some people believe that psychics are merely good guessers, making hundreds of off-hand or vague predictions, and then putting meaning to their 'impressions' when factual evidence surfaces. I believe that this is true in many cases. When Karan investigates a haunt, she has only a few detailed impressions, each of which has specific meaning.

In general I never tell Karan where we are going in advance, or anything about the history of a place. Often I do not know the details behind a supposed haunting myself before we get there. I have confirmed many of Karan's detailed impressions using historic records or witness statements during later research. Not all of Karan's impressions have been 100 percent accurate, but far more than if she were merely guessing.

We walked south on First Avenue, past Ankeny Square, and continued walking toward Ash Street. I did not tell her anything about the place as we crossed the street to the east, toward a nook between buildings. I asked Karan to concentrate hard, and open herself up to the place. She told me that there was some kind of force intentionally blocking her. She jokingly asked me if it would hurt. I told her I would catch her if she fell down.

She said she could not get past it. "Something's standing here, standing outside. But it's intentionally blocking me."

"Well, maybe instead of trying to get past, focus on it. What kind of impression are you getting from whatever is blocking you," I suggested.

She concentrated for several seconds, and said in a hesitant voice, "The term, *dark water* is coming through. I am seeing a silhouette, almost sarcophagus shaped, but it is a bright white." She was very confused, and I suggested that she stop, that perhaps we could come back, or as we continued, some of the impressions would become clearer in her mind.

Karan said she wanted to continue. "I see a white shroud, but dark water. And the pain is rigid. I am standing up, but it is afraid to open it, it is afraid to open up," she laughed nervously.

Whatever had happened there was too confusing for Karan to clearly see at that time. This usually happens in places where there has been a lot of activity and stress, like a battlefield, or the site of a natural disaster. We left, but she continued discussing the place with me. Bear in mind, Karan did not know this area was supposed to be a cemetery, either Native American or Pioneer.

The experience was very powerful. "It's like something was shining a light on this. Or it is something that is good, but died of something bad? A combination of dark and light and does not usually confuse me like that. It's like I was blocked." Karan asked, "this doesn't have something to do with an epidemic?"

"Maybe," I replied.

Karan took that as an agreement. "I know that the dark water, that whole thing, is a term that they used for cholera, or a liver..."

"Black water fever, is Ebola," I said.

"Does that make sense, about what we are talking about?" she asked.

I told her that it was a maybe, but I would not supply any details until she finished her observations.

She ended by saying, "It has to do with the sarcophagus. I feel it had something to do with contaminated water." She mentioned now thinking of the sarcophagus as a gravestone, and asked about any cemeteries in the area.

Karan's Comments:

Jeff took me to a place on the sidewalk next to a set of stairs leading down to a basement door, he asked me to just open up and tell him my impressions. The first thing I got was the phrase Dark Water. I saw in my mind's eye a white sarcophagus with a light shining on it from the right. Something was behind the sarcophagus that I couldn't see. A few minutes later the words contaminated water came to my mind.

A. Dark water for me means a contagious disease.

B. Sarcophagus, coffin or box means containment.

C. The light shining on it making it white and coming from the right means this containment is a good thing.

D. Last, the disease was carried in contaminated water

My friend David spoke with an archaeologist familiar with downtown Portland. She said that a Pioneer graveyard might exist, but it was some distance away from the street corner where Karan and I stopped. She also told David that she thought any Indian graveyard would be somewhere else entirely. This is not the final word on the matter.

Archaeologists frequently hide the location of Native American burial grounds, as part of the Native American Graves Protection and Repatriation Act (NAGPRA.) That is because in the past, when people learned the location of graveyards, some of them went out and robbed the graves. Therefore, even though the archaeologist told David that a Cemetery was somewhere else, it could have been exactly where Karan felt it was. Or it really could have been somewhere else. Of course, when information is guarded too closely, some graveyards might be destroyed by accident.

David mentioned there was a small Pioneer church somewhere in old-town Portland, it surely had a cemetery. No one knows exactly where that was located either. So, there is no more proof for or against a cemetery existing near the site where we stopped. The thing about legends is, there is usually a kernel of truth in them somewhere.

The nineteenth century was a vastly different world than we live in today. A cholera outbreak claiming a small part of a city's population was not worth the newspapers of the time writing about. In 1890, newspapers described the conditions that Portlanders lived in. The Willamette River usually flooded twice a year, and the water settled in basements of the buildings lining the waterfront. The sewers backed up, became a breeding ground for mosquitoes, and the organisms that caused both typhus and cholera. This situation lasted for decades before the City contained the worst of the problem by building flood "sea" walls.

Even if we did not find Portland's Pioneer cemeteries, they are out there. Portland's oldest known cemetery is Lone Fir, which opened in 1866. It was on the east bank of the Willamette River, while other later ones opened south of Portland. What happened to the churches and accompanying graveyards from Portland's first years?

South Old Town Portland

Some of Portland's Pioneers used compasses to set up a magnetic north-south street plan. Others ignored north arros and laid out their roads using the course of the Willamette River. That is why Portland roads jog and change directions at certain points, like where Stark and Oak Streets meet Burnside at nearly 45 degree angles. Burnside itself turns slightly past 14th Avenue for the same reason, as three different street plans come together within a four block area.

Modern Portland is divided into neighborhoods, such as the Pearl District, the Oldtown/Chinatown, Skidmore-Oldtown, etc. These neighborhoods are not the same as existed in the past. For instance, Chinatown originally extended from north of Davis Street all the way south of Washington Street. What I am calling "South Old Town Portland" is roughly a square, containing everything south of West Burnside, from Front Street to SW 14th Avenue, all the way down to SW Harrison.

The Crystal Ballroom

In 1873, John Couch subdivided his property into parcels and oriented his parcel with the Willamette River. When the roads joining Couch's property were built using magnetic north lines, they met at odd angles. This affected the design and the acoustics of the Crystal Ballroom built by Montrose Ringler, nearly 40 years later.

In the late 1800s, Montrose Ringler was a famous dance instructor. His clientele included many of the upper classes, many of whom refused to come to Ringler's school, in a less than savory part of town. In 1913, Ringler approached Paul Van Fridagh with a proposal to build a large dance hall, music school and society center on Van Fridagh's property. It was a risky venture.

In 1913 Lola Baldwin, a local Suffragette and reformer, opposed dancing and dance halls. She believed that music like jazz, dancing, and liquor led to immoral conduct. Baldwin and her coalition were so successful that the City of Portland initiated a temperance ordinance three years before Prohibition became a national law. They also spurred the city to pass four anti-dance ordinances and hire regulators to monitor the dance halls located within Portland.

Even so, Ringler convinced Van Fridagh to back his plan. In January of 1914, Cotillion Hall as the Crystal Ballroom was first known, opened for business. Its main attraction was a "floating" dance floor. This was made of a layer of maple planks laid on top of wooden rocker panels, which had ball bearings attached to the ends of the rockers. This added a gentle swaying motion to the whole floor as people danced. Workers adjusted the rocking motion with a series of gears that changed the floating motion for different dances. The Crystal Ballroom's floor may be the only one of this kind left in the United States.

In 1921, Ringler sold his lease to Cotillion Hall, which fell under less inspired management, after Paul Van Fridagh died in 1925. The building was renamed the Crystal Ballroom in 1950. One of the effects of the lopsided square shape of the Crystal Ballroom is several "dead spots," where patrons have a hard time hearing music. Because of that, and the construction of large auditoriums, the old hall could not compete for popular bands. The Crystal Ballroom closed as a music venue in 1968 and was not reopened until 1997 when McMenamins brought it back to life.

Ed Lawrence was the manager of the Crystal Ballroom in 1998. One night, he and another employee were working late, one floor down from the dance floor. Ed was looking through a filing cabinet near the open doorway. He glanced up at a noise outside the room, and saw a man walk by him, heading toward his office. It was very late and there was not supposed to be anyone in the building. Ed stepped outside the room to investigate. The hallway was empty. It was perhaps 12 feet long. Ed checked all of the offices lining the hallway, making sure they were locked and empty. They were.

For his part, the other man saw Ed look up, walk into the hallway and return a moment later looking puzzled. This man had not seen the figure, but he trusted Ed's word. They both left early that night.

Christmas Eve was not a good night for Ed either. He had company at his house when he received a call from the Crystal Ballroom's security. The burglar alarms had gone off. Ed drove through a snowstorm to the Crystal Ballroom. The police were not there, so he entered alone. He walked up to the second floor, where the stairs lead to the ballroom. Ed wanted to surprise any intruders, so he did not turn on the lights. He got a flashlight and walked up the performer's stairwell. He let himself into the ballroom through a small door. There was no one there. He walked through the ballroom and headed down the main stairs to the second floor.

Ed paused at the foot of the stairs, searching his pockets for the keys to his office. Suddenly he heard the voices of at least seven people talking very loudly, at the top of the stairs above him. Their footsteps and voices grew fainter as they walked into the ballroom. Ed did not feel like investigating this time. Even in the dark, there was no way that many people could have followed Ed across the creaky dance floor without his hearing them. Whether they were ghosts or thrill seekers, there were too many of them for Ed's tastes. He left.

Hotel Vintage Plaza

I received an email about the Hotel Vintage Plaza, which I posted on my website.

At the Hotel Vintage Plaza - managed by Kimpton, in downtown Portland, I experienced moaning in my room on two separate nights (first time a woman, second time a man). On the same evening I heard the man moaning, minutes afterwards, my bed began to shake left to right (it wasn't a violent shake). When my story was told to the night auditor, he said they got that 'complaint' several times...the bed shaking for no reason.
Jim C

It is always interesting when I get a referral like this. Ordinary folk do not mention the management company in their stories. I tried contacting Jim for more details, but did not get a response. I spoke with hotel staffer, Mariane M., on May 3rd, 2007. She said that in the past, nearly the whole block where the Hotel Vintage Plaza stands was part of the Imperial Hotel. Over time, elements of the hotel complex were sold off. She believed that these areas were haunted.

Thomas Guinean built the Imperial Hotel in 1895. He charged $1 a night for a European style room plan, or $2 for an American; which was the same room, but included meals. The Imperial suffered damage and was renovated in 1908. Sometime after that, Guinean sold the hotel to prominent Portland hostlers, the Metschans family. In 1950, the Gentner family bought the hotel, following their purchase of the Mallory Hotel in the 1940s. They owned it until the Imperial Hotel became another casualty of September 11th 2001. People did not travel that year, and the hotel lost many customers, forcing the Gentners to sell it in 2002.

The new owners divided the building into the hotels Vintage Plaza and St. Lucia. The Hotel Lucia and bar occupy what was the Imperial's stables. Marianne told me that a very friendly cat lived in the stables, catching mice. Unfortunately, some joker thought it would be funny to tie a string to the cat's tail. By the time a hotel employee untied the string, the circulation had been cut off too long, and the tail died. The cat caught gangrene and died in the stables. Employees and guests on the ground floor of the Hotel Lucia and bar see it from time to time. Bar patrons also reported seeing a ghostly lady dressed in an older style green dress.

The Green Lady

A few years before the hotel sold, the bartender at the Imperial Bar saw a woman in a green hoop skirt, carrying a parasol, in the bar. It was after closing, but a customer was a customer. Without thinking, he said, "I will be with you in a minute."

He turned away, and did a double take, as he realized how oddly she was dressed. When he turned back, the woman was gone. He was afraid of being ridiculed, and did not talk to anyone about the incident.

Later, another employee saw the same apparition. The woman wore a green, velvety dress, and she was looking out of a window. When the employee confronted her, she smiled and vanished. Like the bartender, this employee did not speak to anyone about the incident for quite a while. When he did, he mentioned it to the owner, Mr. Gentner. Gentner pulled out an old newspaper article from the 1950s, about a woman in green haunting the hotel. The story went round, and the bartender came forward with his story.

Mariane thought that after the renovation at the Hotel Vintage Plaza, paranormal things settled down a bit. No one reported seeing the woman or ghostly cat. Perhaps any spirits went away with the older materials removed during the remodel. She was not quite correct.

In June 2007, I visited the Hotel Vintage Plaza and spoke with several employees at the Concierge Desk. The week prior, a woman called the hotel about her stay in Room 306, while traveling with her child. The woman woke up in the middle of the night, after hearing the voice of her child from the crib. It was routine, children mumble in their sleep, except that the mother heard an adult voice. The mother sat up, looked at the crib, and saw a female form bending over the child. She heard the woman saying, "Be quiet now, your mother will be here in a minute," in a foreign accent.

The mother jumped out of bed and the form disappeared. The woman waited a week to call back with the story. Perhaps she thought she had some kind of nightmare. If so, other guests had their own odd dreams.

Another guest was sleeping in her room when she woke up suddenly. She heard a creaking sound in her room, as if someone was walking across the floor. The creaking stopped, and the television turned on. She got up and turned the television off. A few minutes later, she heard the creaking sound, and the television turned on again. The woman turned the television off again, but it stayed off that time.

Another guest checked into a room on the ninth floor. She went upstairs, put her luggage on the bed, except for her makeup kit, which she put in the bathroom. She went back into the bedroom; and a few seconds later heard a scuffling noise from the bathroom. She investigated, and found that her makeup bag was tipped sideways, and all of her makeup containers were turned upright, on-end. She tried calling the front desk, but her phone was not working. She went down to the lobby, and had the desk clerk investigate.

When the two of them went to the ninth floor, her key did not work. He tried his master key, but it did not work either. They got the master keys from the front desk, and none of them unlocked the door. Finally, they tried the original room key, and the door opened. The woman demanded a new room. The desk clerk did not blame her, and got her a room on the fourth floor. He helped gather all of her luggage and took it down there. One thing she did not find when she checked out was her hairbrush.

The night auditor thought she might have left it in either room, or lost it in the elevator or hallway when she moved. The woman was that upset. He took the description of the brush, and posted it for all hotel staff to keep an eye out for it. An hour and a half later, the housekeeping staff found her brush in a locked room on the third floor. The spirits of the hotel did not just play tricks on the guests.

One night, an employee named Brian was inside a fourth floor linen closet, taking inventory. He felt like someone was watching him. He looked around, but did not see anyone. He went back to work, and the feeling returned. He stopped, turned around, and saw the shadowy form of a little boy, watching him from around a corner. Brian had a confused impression of an off-white outfit with stripes. As Brian walked toward the boy, he ran around the corner. It only took a few seconds for Brian to reach the corner and look around it, but the boy had vanished.

Part of the duties of the night auditor were to walk through the public areas in the hotel at regular intervals. Acting as the night auditor, Brian went into the basement to check on things. He paused outside the exercise room, after seeing the television playing inside through the glass doors. It was not set on a single channel. Instead, the television picture was moving on fast forward, strobing from station to station .

He went inside to turn the television off, but paused because the room was very cold. He thought someone had left the air conditioner on. He checked the thermostat, which registered a heat of 80 degrees or so. It felt more like 45 or 50 degrees. He turned the television off, and left the room. He paused a few feet away, by a set of pay phones (now gone.)

He heard a noise behind him, and reflected on the wall in front of him, Brian saw the same strobe-like flicker of a television on fast forward. He went back to the exercise room to turn the television off again. This time; each time the television changed channel, it put out the sound from each station. This was unusual, if not impossible. Televisions on fast forward do not normally carry the sound. Brian had had enough at that point. He went back to the main lobby and told one of the other staff to check out the basement. The man returned a few minutes later, after turning off the television himself, only to have it come back on again as well.

The Woman at the US Bank Tower?

It is interesting how stories are dismissed as urban legends, to be proven true, or partly true later. I have a friend who worked at the U.S. Bank Tower, which was built in 1983, and she told me this story.

A knife wielding man in the lobby attacked a woman several years ago. She made it into the elevator and got off on the fifth floor, to hide from her attacker. People riding the elevator in the evenings will be surprised when the elevator stops on the fifth floor automatically.

She did not have many more details, or confirmation from the building management. I checked online newspaper accounts, searching for any such incidents. There were stories of shootings nearby, but no details of a woman attacked inside. My resources only went back about 20 years, Apparently, this story had an even older origin.

Like most people, I did not realize that the U.S. Bancorp, which is headquartered in Minnesota, has its origins in Portland. It began as the United States National Bank of Portland, founded in 1891. In 1964, it changed into the U.S. National Bank of Oregon, and after a series of mergers, the resulting mega-bank adopted the name of U.S Bancorp in 1997. In going back to the bank's origins, I learned more.

My friend David put me in touch with Tom Carrollo the manager of the old U.S. Bank building, on Stark and 6th Avenue. This building is sometimes confused with the U.S. Bankcorp Tower a few blocks away, though it is much older, dating to the early 1900s. It is only five stories high, as opposed to the nearby 43 storey tower. I met with Tom in June 2007, and as we spoke, we walked through the building, speaking with several other employees along the way.

On the eve of World War I, the American banking industry was expanding, and the U.S. Bank wanted to show its prominence and trustworthiness. Their design encompassed most of the block. The first floor of the building still has the high ceilings, as well as the revolving door entrances. Their design took up most of the block, but the owners could not obtain the entire block at once. So they built the bank in stages. The first section, (the eastern half) was begun in 1915, and finished in 1917. The second section, (the western half) was built between 1925 and 1926. The builders did their work so well that it is hard to tell where the original half ends, and the new half begins.

Today the first floor houses a branch of the U.S. Bancorp, which has some symmetry. Perhaps the confusion between the old and new buildings includes the ghostly woman and her haunted elevator. As we walked through the marble tiled lobby, Tom told me a legend repeated by bank employees. Many decades ago, the bank was robbed, and one of the tellers, Martha was wounded. She fled onto the elevator, where she died. They think that this happened in the 1920s, but no one has had time to research the newspapers, and confirm the story one way or another.

There were actually two elevators, side by side and Tom and I rode one up to the third floor. We paused to look at some historic photographs of the building. We returned to the elevators, and paused continuing our conversation. We heard the elevator bell ding, and both elevators stopped on our floor. Their doors opened, as if asking us to get in… not that we or anyone else pushed the elevator buttons.

We rode an elevator down to the ground floor, and walked down to the basement. One of the engineers, Bob, reported that he had been working there, when he felt a presence, and something invisible touched him on the shoulder. The tunnels under the building did not resemble the "Shanghai" tunnels, they were more modern, with concrete walls, heating ducts, electrical conduit, etc. In one place, the floor changed from concrete to marble. In the past, it had been office space. Tom showed me a bank vault, and said that the Rose Festival crown was kept there when not used.

We never found Bob, but spoke with Ian, his assistant. Several times he and Bob worked on the elevators, following complaints that they moved up and down on their own. He said that there was nothing mechanical or electrically wrong with them. Once he was in the elevator shaft looking at the switches, when one tripped on its own, even though no one had pressed the call button from the outside. Fortunately, he was not in the way of the moving elevator.

We returned to the main floor and found one of the bank guards, named Harry. He had an interesting incident on his first day on the job, in 1999. He was on the ground floor, looking around. He was in an empty backroom, when he saw a door open and close on its own, as if someone had entered or left the empty room. Harry admitted that the door could have been blown open on its own, but what could have caused it to swing closed? Harry did not want anyone thinking he was crazy on his first day, so he pretended it did not happen. He did not mention it until my visit.

Harry was not the only one to notice strange things. The main entrance is through a set of old fashioned revolving doors. These keep drafts out, but they also keep people in wheelchairs outside. So the building owner paid for new ones

to be installed. Harry spoke with one of the workmen installing the doors. He told Harry that one morning, he and another man heard footsteps walking down the stairs from an upper floor, toward them on the ground floor. Although the steps looked like marble, they were actually wood, and the echo was distinctive. They paused, wondering who was in the building so early.

The footsteps got louder as the person came closer, then

suddenly stopped. The person should have been visible, but the workmen never saw anyone. It scared the workers, who heard that shortly after the building was completed, one of the female employees, named Martha had a heart attack and died while walking down those stairs. Was this a case of two legends, two tragic deaths, or just coincidence?

The Benson Hotel

Simon Benson was born in Norway in 1851, and originally named Simon Berger Iversen. When he emigrated to the United States in 1867, he compressed the family name to Benson. Benson came to the Pacific Northwest in 1880, where he opened his own lumber business, but sold it in 1883, when his wife became ill. Following her death in 1890, Benson resumed his lumber business, introducing steam-powered trains to move logs from the forest to his mills. He pioneered the use of oceangoing log rafts to transport raw lumber from the Oregon to California.

Benson had an interesting mix of business sense as well as down-to-earth common sense. He was angry when he heard that the saloons lining Portland's waterfront would not serve water to patrons, only alcoholic drinks. Many of the men lured into the saloons worked for Benson, and this hurt his business when they were hung over the next day. Rumor has it that Benson himself asked for a drink of water in a bar, and the owners threw him out. Benson paid to install 20 free drinking fountains in downtown Portland. Some of them are still operating, and called the "Benson Bubblers."

In 1909, Simon Benson sold many of his land holdings and

invested in the development of Portland. He endowed schools, built roads, and donated hundreds of acres of land for Portland parks. He and other Portland entrepreneurs wanted to show the rest of the world that Portland was a major cultural center. They built the Oregon Hotel in 1912, but after 16 months of losing money, Benson took control of the business and renamed it the Benson Hotel.

Benson hired Portland architect Albert Doyle to design the French Empire style hotel that eventually bore his name. Doyle's design was inspired by Chicago's Blackstone Hotel. The building had 12 stories, with a terracotta and brick exterior. It had a French mansard roof with dormers. Many guests entering the hotel are impressed with the glass-and-steel marquee set above the hotel's main entrance. It replaced the original marquee, which fell under the weight of snow in the winter of 1937. Inside the hotel lobby, Doyle used Italian marble floors, and Circassian walnut paneling with Austrian crystal chandeliers. The overall effect was to outshine the European style hotels in Seattle and San Francisco.

In 1991, the hotel restaurant, the London Grill underwent a massive remodel, which may have energized the hidden spirits. One of the chefs threatened to quit when items he put down in the kitchen disappeared, only to reappear in a different place. Other service staff felt a presence following them around the kitchen. One employee even saw a shadowy figure walking down the hallway. Most of the sightings happened in the back of the restaurant, and stopped after the remodel. Others did not.

The hotel used to have an old-fashioned live-operator switchboard, which faced away from the only door leading into the operator's booth. The operator could see the entrance by looking at the reflection in a small mirror on the top of the switchboard. One evening as the operator sat at her station, something in the mirror caught her eye. She saw the door behind her open, and watched a middle-aged man walk in and pause, looking at her. They locked eyes. There was nothing remarkable about him, but he was a stranger.

She turned around to tell the man that guests were not allowed. When she faced the door, there was no one there. She whipped around and looked in the mirror again. The man was still reflected there, staring at her. She did a double take, looking behind her and at the mirror again. She saw the same thing. Empty air behind her, a man reflected in the mirror. Then suddenly he was gone. This happened to her a few more times but she never quit her job.

Hotel employees have seen a woman dressed in white roaming the upper-floor hallways. She may have been an attendant who stayed on at the hotel after her death. In the past, the Benson had an employee on each floor to help guests with problems such as lost room keys, towels, or even help infirm guests into bed. In the late 1990s, an elderly female guest struggled to turn down the covers, when a woman in white came up behind her and helped the guest into bed. The guest thought the woman was the regular floor attendant, alerted by the staff. Once in bed, the guest watched the woman exit the room by walking through the closed door.

Several times guests and employees have seen a tall man dressed in a black coat, walking down the hotel's grand stairway. As he reaches the bottom of the staircase, he disappears. According to one person, the man became transparent and faded as he walked down the stairs. This sighting may have happened in 2004 or 2005. It is unlikely that the man in black was Simon Benson. He moved to Los Angeles in the 1920s, and died there in 1942. Benson then returned to the Pacific Northwest, and he was buried in Portland's Riverview Cemetery.

Who has Joe Hill's ashes?

The Alternate State of Mind is located in the same building where Tom Burns operated his watch shop, on Burnside, between 2nd and 3rd Avenue. Tom Burns and a man named Joe Hill shared a macabre national incident that has its origins in Portland.

Tom Burns was a recruiter for the International Workers of the World, the IWW, also known to their enemies as the Wobblies. The IWW was a grassroots labor movement whose aim was to overthrow the "capitalist class.' Although many IWW members read Karl Marx, the IWW viewed itself as a homegrown society of laborer liberators. Joe Hill, a laborer, poet, singer and songwriter was one of their heroes.

Hill joined the IWW twice. On his first application he listed his enrollment place as Portland, Oregon, which meant Tom Burns' watch shop. In 1910, Hill wrote an article for the *Industrial Worker*, and in it, he identified himself as a member of the Portland IWW. Hill soon moved on, and made his way to Utah, where he organized several labor strikes in the 1900s.

In January 1914, a masked man shot and killed a Salt Lake City grocer and his son. In the robbery, the grocer shot the robber. Soon after that, Hill went to a local hospital with a gunshot wound. As the only suspect, he went on trial for the murder, and was convicted. There was an international outcry for his release, or at least to have his death sentence commuted, but to no avail. On November 15, 1915, Joe Hill was executed by firing squad.

Hill became a martyr and a symbol of the IWW movement. After a memorial ceremony at their headquarters in Chicago, the IWW cremated Hill. They divided his ashes, putting them into hundreds of coin envelopes, each bearing Hill's final poem and photograph. They sent these packets to IWW offices in the United States, and around the world.

The IWW held local memorial services for Hill, spreading his ashes in their halls, or on the ground outside. Some kept Hill's ashes as an heirloom. Tom Burns probably got several packets to give to IWW organizers across Oregon. Perhaps he kept them in a glass jar, or some other small vessel on display in the shop. Oddly, the U.S. Government confiscated one packet of ashes as seditious material.

The ashes eventually went into the National Archives, until 1988, when the head of the 300 member strong IWW petitioned the government for their return. They got the ashes, but not the envelope. They kept Joe Hill in a jar, which they bring out and put on display, to enhearten the remaining Industrial Workers of the World. When Tom Burns left the shop, did the ashes remain hidden somewhere? The workers at the Alternate State of Mind do not know… or do they?

Dan and Louis Oyster Bar

In 1907, Louis Wachsmuth started selling raw oysters on Portland's docks. His brother Dan later became an employee and partner. In 1919, Louis bought the Merchant's Exchange Saloon, and his principal dish was Oyster Stew, from his own recipe. It must have been good, because his restaurant got bigger. The largest addition included a ship style extension built in 1937. If ever a place deserved to be haunted by a devoted owner or employee, it is Dan and Louis Oyster Bar. I spoke with "Tuck" Wachsmuth in 2007, about ghosts at the Oyster Bar. He informed me that they did not have any reluctant ghosts, but I still recommend stopping by.

Dan and Louis restaurant resembles some of the modern Yuppie bars where the wall hangings are reproductions of antique maritime artifacts. Except the wall hangings at Dan and Louis are real antiques. Celebrity pictures, some dating to the 1950s hang on the walls. The windows are shaped like round portholes and the wooden walls are hung with ship models, ropes, and old pictures of past employees and the seacoast.

One historically tragic piece of memorabilia at Dan and Louis Oyster Bar is the ship's wheel from the *Brother Jonathan*. The *Brother Jonathan* was built in 1851, in a time when ships used steam power, but builders included wind sails, just in case. She was 220' long, and 36' wide, with two masts, but her main propulsion came from two 33-foot side-mounted paddle wheels. *Brother Jonathan* carried passengers as well as cargo, in two, 70' long salons, decorated with gold leaf and enamel, as well as passenger cabins.

The *Brother Jonathan* made many trips taking gold miners and their equipment from California to Alaska. The owners wanted to earn as much money as possible, regardless of the risk. In 1865, the *Brother Jonathan* collided with a ship on the Columbia River, damaging her hull. The captain had a patch put on her hull, and returned to San Francisco on 27 July. The Company Agent ordered her to sail north without repair. He also loaded the ship with more cargo and passengers. The stevedores placed an ore crusher, weighing several tons, over the spot where the hull was patched. Despite his misgivings, the Captain finished loading.

Before the *Brother Jonathan* sailed, U.S. Army officer, Major Eddy boarded with the pay for all of the soldiers stationed in the Northwestern Region. He was probably carrying paper money, but it could have included gold coins. If it were all gold, $200,000 would have weighed about 4,000 ounces. In addition to Eddy, the Indian Agents also sent a shipment of gold coins to pay local tribes their annual settlements. There is no telling how much other gold was onboard. There were rumors that Well's Fargo also had a gold shipment for their Oregon and Washington operations. At midday on the 28th, the *Brother Jonathan* cast off her lines from the San Francisco piers, and steamed out of the Bay. The ship fought a strong headwind, and the heavy seas caused most of the passengers to go to their cabins, seasick.

On the afternoon of July 30, the *Brother Jonathan* headed north, after pausing to drop off cargo in Crescent City, California. A storm came up, and the captain decided to return to Crescent City. As the ship headed around St. George Reef, a heavy wave carried her onto a partially submerged rock, which jutted up from the sea floor, 250 feet below. The waves pushed the ship across the rocky outcrop, which like a can opener tore the ship's bottom apart. The ore crusher fell through the deck, as the ship began sinking. The captain ordered everyone to abandon ship, but they could not launch the lifeboats. A ship's officers managed to load a smaller boat with 18 passengers and crew, which made it away. These were the only survivors.

The storm kept rescue parties away from the *Brother Jonathan* for two days. When they arrived, all they found was floating wreckage. They named the submerged monolith Jonathan Rock. A tragic piece of wreckage was the wheel of the *Brother Jonathan*. The ship's wheel symbolizes strength, purpose, and direction, as the captain and crew steer the ship through calm and stormy seas. Finding the wheel after a

wreck also symbolizes the frail nature of humanity when compared to the unpredictable nature of the sea. Even more tragic, in a last ditch effort to save the ship, one man lashed himself to the wheel. The rescuers found his body still tied to it, when they recovered the wheel.

The *Brother Jonathan's* wheel eventually came to rest in Dan and Louis Oyster Bar, near the main entrance. No one has reported that the wheel is haunted. However, it is hard to believe that a little bit of the tragedy does not still cling to it today. Knowing this story, a few brave souls touch the wheel, sending a blessing for peace for all who went down with the *Brother Jonathan*. To those skeptics who do not believe, perhaps they will want to touch it to prove that there is no such thing as bad luck, and hope their skepticism will not upset any spirits of the past.

The Brother Jonathan's cargo

In the 1930s, a fisherman found 22 pounds of gold bars, bearing a mintmark of 1865. He died before he told anyone where the gold came from, but everyone supposed it came from the *Brother Jonathan*. Sonar located the wreck under 250 feet of water, below the depth most commercial divers could reach. For many years various people laid claim to the gold bars, until they eventually reached a settlement. In 1993, divers reached the *Brother Jonathan* and recovered several coins, which sparked a lawsuit between the treasure hunters and the government, which continued for several years. Eventually the State of California and the salvagers settled, and sold a thousand gold coins, and archaeologists are now recovering the rest of the *Brother Jonathan*.

Kell's Irish Pub

Kell's Irish Pub is located near Chinatown, and the "Shanghai" tunnels that connected most of old Portland run through its basement. Even though Kell's is a smoke free bar, this does not apply to the basement, which has a cigar bar. The cigar bar really does look like it belongs in an Irish pub. The ceiling is low and the floor is uneven concrete and tile. The walls are hung with Irish theme prints. Strangely, a ghostly Shanghaied old-time sailor does NOT haunt Kell's.

Kell's is an interesting place; nice people, good food and drink. However, in the late 1800s, there was a warehouse explosion and fire nearby. It traveled from business to business through the tunnels. According to stories, the cigar room in the basement of Kell's is part of a portion of a tunnel that collapsed, injuring a fireman, who later died of smoke inhalation. Psychics visiting Kell's told the manager that they have felt the presence of a firefighter in the pub. Patrons have seen a firefighter, dressed in his old-fashioned hat and jacket in the basement. He usually disappears before anyone can confront him. One of the bartenders was in the basement and he felt someone tap his shoulder. When he turned around there was no one there.

In 2007, I visited Kell's with my clairvoyant friend Karan. She developed a headache. She told me that he sensed she was in the upper floor, and wanted her to come down. Karan said, "I would like to eat lunch without feeling like my head's being crushed."

If she did not come down to acknowledge him, he would increase the pressure. So, we went down to the cigar bar basement, where the ghost was. After a short visit, and chat with the spirit, we went back to the main floor and had our lunch. I think I had the corned beef and cabbage.

In 2003, I received an email about Kell's

A very spooky haunting as a patron of Kell's pub a few years ago. I had just arrived at Kell's on a weekday evening to meet friends. We headed down to the smoking room to share a cigarette and avoid the crowd. Shortly after arriving, I excused myself for a trip to the ladies room. I headed down the long hallway to the women's restroom. A heavy wooden door allowed access to the room inside. I found a sink straight ahead

of me, and two stalls.

I was alone, so I simply chose the first stall. Almost as immediately, as I had entered the stall, a terrible and frantic pounding began beating on my stall door with a frightening urgency. I had thought it strange for someone to be beating on my door with an open stall right next to me, but as I looked straight ahead there was no one in the room. The heavy wooden door would not have been able to open and shut without my noticing, and I found myself frozen with fear as the doors rattled and shook with every forceful pound.

I finally raced out of the bathroom, back down the long hallway and met up with my friends in the smoking room. With tears in my eyes, I relayed the story of the urgent pounding only to find faces of disbelief. I asked a waitress upstairs if strange things were know to happen in the basement and she replied "oh, did something happen to you in the basement? I refuse to work down there alone"

The pounding on the door is unforgettable. Perhaps the same sort of pounding that a firefighter might use to warn or alert someone? (My father was a firefighter) I have returned to the basement a few times. I also have pictures of myself and friends in the smoking room at Kell's with balls of light floating over our heads...

Sincerely, Amy

We exchanged a couple of emails, and I told Amy I believed at the time that the firefighter died in the Depression, which was after the great fire. She emailed back to me.

Hello Jeff!

Just yesterday, I went to lunch with my mother. I was telling her the Kell's ghost story about the firefighter that lost his life. As I spoke her eyes lit up and she told me this story... As she recalled, there has only been one firefighter who lost his life in the line of duty. She knows this because in 1974, my father received a medal for bravery and injury in the line of duty.

"I gave you that medal when your father and I separated, a few years ago, do you still have it?

"I do have that medal... "David Campbell" The medal states that he lost his life in the line of duty on June 26th 1911.

Amy

Did Amy have some kind of connection to the firefighter who haunts the basement at Kell's?

Portland has a *David Campbell* Fire Boat, to fight fires on ships, docks, and buildings lining the Willamette. Built in 1927, it looks very much like a tugboat, but it has powerful pumps, which draw water out of the river, and forces it out of several nozzles mounted on the boat. People can see it during the Rose Festival, spraying colored water out of its nozzles, to welcome the incoming ships

Mama Mia's

Mama Mia's Restaurant is located on the northwest corner of 2nd Avenue and Washington Street. In the past, it was known as the Elephant and Castle, and is haunted in both incarnations. Both restaurants were housed on the first floor of the Waldo Building, built in 1886. Originally, the first floor housed the Merchants National Bank, while the Leeland lodging rooms occupied the second and third floors. In the early 1900s, the upper floors were leased to various Chinese societies who may have engaged in gambling, prostitution, and opium selling, in addition to other social and religious activities. There were five tunnels in the basement, all of which are blocked up.

In the 1960s, George Frederici had the idea to open an English style pub close to the police station. He named it after the "Elephant and Castle Pub" in England. This name dates to the 16th Century, when the Spanish princess, the Infanta de Castile stopped outside London on her way to marry the king. At the inn where she stopped, the locals could not pronounce her title. The best they could do was call her the "Elephant and Castle." The name stuck to the pub built on the site. George ran the bar for several years before passing it on to his daughter Sharon.

People reported feeling a presence at the bar. It centered around a stool, with the name George on it. That was where George Frederici held court for many years. Some years earlier, the woman who ran a hair salon next door, committed suicide in the basement. She may be the person customers heard walking in the back of the bar, where there had been keno machines. Some customers also heard the sound of chairs falling or soft footsteps in the back room.

Sharon showed me a very old stall with walls, ceiling and a locking door made of chicken wire and boards, standing in the center of the basement. She told me that it was filled with dirt and garbage. One day she cleaned up inside and found an opium scale at the bottom of the pile of junk. Her thought was that people did smoke opium in the basement, which they bought from someone in the old stall, using the old scale. This would explain why someone needed to build a semi-secure stall in the basement.

A few years ago, the Elephant and Castle became Mama Mia's restaurant. I visited Mama Mia's with my friend Karan, and spoke with owner, Lisa, who had problems from the moment she decided to open a restaurant there in 2004. While we spoke, Karan walked through the building with one of the employees, Amanda. Before we got there, Karan told me there was something *off* about the lighting.

It took several months to turn the Elephant and Castle into Mama Mia's. Lisa put her kitchen where the Elephant and Castle had their dart room. Once they started work, Lisa learned that the floor joists were all rotten. It was too late to find

another location so she had to replace them, which increased her costs. One piece of the old Elephant and Castle that is left at Mama Mia's was the bar.

The men who put in the floor around it did not seal it properly. Now any water spilled at the bar somehow finds its way through the floor into the basement.

Lisa wanted to put her best foot forward, spiritual wise. Before she opened Mama Mia's, Lisa smudged the restaurant with herbs, to quiet any spirits. She also held a Feng Shui ceremony offering rice wine and tangerine peels. After that, she had a business opportunity that went wrong.

Earlier she tried getting the lease on a photo studio next door. The owner left, and Lisa bought it. When Lisa was renovating Mama Mia's, a very good friend helped her decorate the restaurant. By way of thanks, Lisa suggested converting the old photo shop into a place where he could sell his furniture. He turned it into a combination furniture store, and cafe. They called it the Balaboosta, which was Yiddish for perfect housewife. Coincidentally, this space had been the beauty parlor, run by the woman who committed suicide.

Within a few months, things went sour. Lisa's friend was not happy. Eventually he stopped coming in and their friendship ended. The next manager did not keep business up, so Lisa closed the Balaboosta, after she started having trouble with Mama Mia's. Problems that she had never had before.

Mama Mia's was always full and got good reviews. but it did not make more than a modest profit. She made several changes shortly before my visit. This included firing several employees and a manager who had worked for her for years, after he became unreliable, like her ex-friend.

Ghosts at Mama Mia's?

Lisa had heard ghost stories from the Elephant and Castle folks but treated them with skepticism. During the remodel her own people told her of a few odd stories. Doors were found left open, or closed. A few people reported seeing something on the upper floor, but Lisa did not see anything odd. She was the first to arrive, and the last to leave at the end of the day, and discounted the stories as mistaken impressions or coincidences. Even so she still wondered.

Lisa thought it was weird that the partnership at the Balaboosta, had ended so badly. Someone told Lisa about the previous owner's suicide. Lisa heard she went into the basement below the Balaboosta, and drank herself to death. Lisa wondered if that influence caused her problems. Her employees referred to the basement space below the Balaboosta as the "Scary Room."

At that point in Lisa's interview, Karan returned, and we met in the main dining room. Karan said there was not much activity on the ground floor, except the bathroom. She pointed out that people do not release their emotions in a restaurant dining room. Instead, they go to the bathroom, where they let off steam.

We went into the basement and Karan stopped at a place where there was a broken down wall. She that an entity there caused people in the room above to change their attitudes. This was directly underneath the Balaboosta. Karan took us to another spot, where she felt a pressure spot, and the air was heavier around it. Karan felt that there was a death in that spot sometime in the past.

Lisa asked if Karan had any clue as to how the person died. Karan told her that she felt that there was some kind of feeling of hanging, choking, or feeling tied up. While this suggests strangulation, did the woman who drank herself to death choke on her vomit? Lisa asked about the entity at the end of the basement, below the Balaboosta. She wanted to know if the entity had died in the basement. If not, why was he hanging around? Karan did not know, but said that there was some intelligence behind the spirit, and he did go far from the spot. In life, the man worked down there, and he returned, and wanted to be noticed. The actual man probably died somewhere else, but he left something behind, and still influenced people in or near the basement.

As we left the basement, Lisa asked Karan if Amanda (her walk through guide) told her what they called the basement room where Karan detected the death. Karan replied no. Lisa told her, "the Scary Room." Karan believed that the basement spirit intentionally created some kind of ruse or deception, trying to manipulate people, even after death. We went upstairs next.

Karan said that in the past, the office on the second floor was used as apartments. A janitor who worked at the apartments was with a group of thieves, who got into the rooms (which are now Lisa's business offices,) for illegal purposes. Their activity left an imprint in Lisa's offices.

We went into Lisa's business office. Karan said that the man and woman had lived (separately) in the floors above. Lisa showed us some old fashioned wallpaper hanging on the wall, suggesting that someone might have lived there, or the room had seen better days. There was a back doorway or trapdoor in a connecting room.

Karan sensed two entities in the upper floors, one male and one female. The male was hostile, and she sensed he had an obsession with numbers, hiding numbers, and blaming others. Karan also said that earlier, she heard a woman's voice saying, "it's not my fault."

Karan told us that the man snuck into the office from the trapdoor to do his illegal business, which might have been embezzlement. The woman felt guilty that she did not stop it, and he eventually had her blamed for it. This shame haunted her when she was alive, and caused her to remain. Karan told Lisa that the spirit resented Lisa's business success. However, now that he was exposed, the "numbers guy" was embarrassed. All Lisa had to do was to tell him that the jig was up, and he could either fall in line, or go. Karan suggested that the female spirit was relieved that someone knew she was innocent, and both of them would quiet down..

Amanda mentioned an incident that happened before our visit. One day she set up the business files in a neatly organized pile. When she returned, the files were completely reorganized. She looked for the practical joker, but was alone at the time. Before Amanda told her story, Karan had of course asked about anything messing with the business files.

Later, I listened to the audio recording I made. As Karan, Lisa and I walked upstairs to Lisa's office, I heard Karan tell Lisa that the male spirit should be told to leave. Next I heard a voice, whispering. I believe that it was not my voice, nor Karan's, or Lisa's. The voice was low toned, but audible and it said something like, "then he's gone," or "then I'll go."

Later, Lisa told us the day after we left, she was sitting at her desk, working on the computer, when three books "jumped" or fell off a shelf, and hit her in the arm. Lisa was very precise, she would never put anything on the shelf so that it might fall. She was certain the three books did not fall, it was more like they were aimed at her. Karan told Lisa about the possible spirit voice on the stairs, suggesting that this was the last hurrah of the bad bookkeeper. He let Lisa know that he was gone, but maybe not forever.

The Morrison Bridge

There were unconfirmed reports that the Morrison Bridge was haunted, but no details have surfaced. There was a case where a trolley was crossing one of Portland's many bridges in the past, and it skidded sideways on the icy bridge. I am not certain that this was on the Morrison Bridge, or that anyone died there. However, the Morrison Bridge has an interesting association with Portland's dead.

In ancient Greece, people placed a coin under the tongues of the dead, so they could pay Charon, the ferryman to take them across the River Styx, into the land of the dead. The oldest Portland Cemetery was the Lone Fir, located on the east bank of the Willamette River, which opened in 1866. There was a funeral home near Mama Mia's. The only way to get bodies from this place to Lone Fir was by crossing the Willamette. From the 1860s to 1887, they used a ferry, which docked near Washington Street and Front Avenue. Unlike ancient Greece, in Portland, people paid a ferry toll for pedestrians, horses, and wagons, but the coffins of the dead rode for free. After 1887, the first Morrison Bridge was constructed on the same site, and in the beginning it was also a toll bridge. Hopefully they continued the same practice, otherwise it should have been named the Charon Bridge.

The Heathman Hotel

The Heathman Hotel, with its Italian Renaissance façade and gorgeous décor was built in 1927. It was not just a stopping point for travelers. It was a place for Portland's wealthy to mix in a rich, cultured atmosphere. It was built as a showpiece for the world to see the financial and social prestige of the city of Portland.

The builders used exotic woods from all over the world for the many public rooms. Unfortunately, in the 1950s, people stopped staying in luxury hotels, in favor of the convenience of the motor inns. The Heathman began to suffer during an exodus of businesses and people from downtown Portland in the 1950s and 60s.

The hotel was renovated in 1998, in grand style. High Tea is served every day at 2 PM in the eucalyptus paneled Tea Court. Forty-eight of the Heathman's rooms face a mural artist Henk Pander painted on the wall of the Arlene Schnitzer Concert Hall. The paintings that decorate the Heathman's lobby are classics, ranging from 18th century European masters, to Andy Warhol silk-screens. The Heathman's library has several books signed by authors who stopped at the Heathman. Despite the upgrades the original Heathman is still recognizable, this may be why a resident ghosts remain.

Most of the paranormal activity in the hotel seems to be centered around Room 703. No one has ever seen who, or what has occupied the room, but they see the effects. Many guests check into the room, unpack and go about their business. When they return, they sometimes find a half filled glass of water on the desktop. Sometimes the chair at the desk has been shifted, as if someone moved it to sit down. At other times a towel in the bathroom is removed from the bar, and put on the counter, as if someone used it. Most guests call the front desk to complain. This is how the hotel staff knows that this has been going on for several years.

The hotel has twice a day maid service, and some guests blamed it on the staff. It is easy to believe that a careless maid created a small mess instead of cleaning up. The hotel staff of course blamed the mess on forgetful guests or intruders who somehow entered the room. This changed when the hotel installed electronic locks on each room. The locks record how many times a door was opened, and at what time. Now when a guest in Room 703 calls the front desk and complains, the concierge can take a reading of how many times the door has been opened. In all of the strange cases reported by guests, the electronic record shows that no one has entered the room besides the guest.

A guest, who was also a psychic, talked to management after staying in Room 703. She told them that she had seen a ghost standing at the foot of her bed. She concluded that the spirit energy was concentrated vertically in the hotel, in a line from Room 303 to 1003. Her theory is that a guest of the hotel had committed suicide by jumping out of a window, and was haunting the rooms he passed on his way down the side of the building.

Other people have heard the sound of whispering voices in the same hallways. Then there is the sound of disembodied footsteps walking down the grand staircase. It seems that there is a lot to see, hear, and feel at the Heathman.

North Old Town Portland

As Portland transitioned from the 19th to the 20th century, architecture as well as social values changed. Portland suffered many fires and floods in its early days, and rebuilt itself many times. Ornate brick and cast-iron front buildings replaced the first wooden buildings.

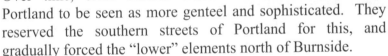

These in turn were replaced by modest brick and steel buildings that reflected a more utilitarian view. Portland was a wild open town, where hard-working, hard-drinking sailors, lumberjacks, and laborers mixed, and gambling and prostitution were openly flaunted. Over time, civic leaders wanted Portland to be seen as more genteel and sophisticated. They reserved the southern streets of Portland for this, and gradually forced the "lower" elements north of Burnside.

Portland had many hotels, ranging from luxurious to the simply furnished. Most of the better hotels were near the train station, or south of Burnside. In between these locales, were cheaper hotels, where a room might cost 50 cents a night for little more than a cot. North of Burnside was the place where most working-class men and women found their lodging. Restaurants, bars, or shops usually occupied hotel ground floors, while travelers stayed in "cribs," little ten by ten foot rooms on the upper floors. Most of these buildings were three or four stories high, with no elevators.

The Barracuda, aka Erickson's Saloon

The heart of Portland's edgy culture was the *Blazing Center*, which included Second and Third Avenues, and Couch and Burnside Streets. Perhaps the best known bar within the Blazing Center was Erickson's Saloon, known today as the Barracuda.

The longest description of Erickson's Saloon comes from *Wildmen, Wobblies & Whistle Punks*, by Brian Booth. Erickson's Saloon sounds like a jolly place, where working stiffs got together in a friendly environment. True, there was a little roughhousing, supervised by professional but jolly bouncers. But it was all in good fun, presided over by the professor-like Gus Erickson. Some of this was true, but some of it was probably not.

Where August "Gus" Erickson came from is still something of a mystery. He owned a "notorious" saloon on 7th and Astor Street in Astoria, and moved to Portland in 1890, and opened a bar, which some people called the *Nine Bar Saloon*. It had nine different bars inside and when added together their length totaled 684 feet. The building itself covered half the block, and the saloon took up two stories, though there was a third floor where there was probably gambling and prostitution. An annex known as Erickson's Hotel, was built onto the saloon. This and the saloon's third floor were used as cribs for transient workers.

Erickson was into self-promotion, and offering something new to his patrons. Erickson used the title *Working Men's Club*, along with the "Dainty Lunch," on his business card. He hosted a large free lunch, which was free so long as you kept drinking, which might not be too hard, at five cents a pint. His saloon had the best of everything, including a very expensive pipe organ, mirrors and electric lights, his magnificent buffet, and imported as well as domestic beer. There were other interesting innovations.

In traditional saloons, women customers were not allowed inside. Instead, Erickson had a series of booths built near the entrance, to allow women to sit, but still be safe from drunken workmen. According to one source, Erickson had women dance on a first floor stage, which he surrounded with an electric fence to keep drunks away. Erickson issued aluminum tokens instead of cash as change, which were good at either of his saloons. That kept his customers loyal.

In 1894, Portland suffered a flood, which covered over 250 square blocks and the first floor of the buildings lining Front Street were under water. Erickson rented a large boat, and stocked it with liquor. He had people in rowboats and canoes bring thirsty customers to his floating bar. They say a few patrons did not leave until the flood waters receded completely. Of course, in addition to drinking, prostitution, and gambling, there were rumors of shanghaiing. According to one source, Erickson's alone had a half dozen trapdoors in the first floor.

The first Portland policeman to be killed in the line of duty was murdered in Erickson's Saloon. According to this source, the policeman had entered the bar, chasing a robber. He was ambushed by a mob of the thief's friends. According to another person, he went into the bar to rescue a woman who was a police informant as well as a prostitute.

Prohibition did not kill Erickson's Saloon, but it slowed things down. The saloon owners complied with the anti-alcohol law and served near-beer in the bar, at least in front. They and other establishments generally moved the beer barrels into back rooms or upstairs. Once Prohibition ended Erickson's re-opened, but could not sell hard liquor. As the years wore on, the owners refused to refurbish the aging bar. Eventually the world's largest bar was dismantled, as the owners tore down old walls and put up new ones, creating more rental space. Erickson's continued in a reduced size, with an aging clientele for many decades. In the 1990s, the building was sold and refurbished, and turned to its present use as the Barracuda Club.

Clairvoyant description of Erickson's Saloon

In April 2007, Karan and I stopped outside the Barracuda. Neither of us knew the history of the building. It was closed, but we *admired* posters for the Paris Hilton Look-Alike contest. Even from outside, Karan had some impressions. She felt that two men had fought on a stairway, and one killed the other, or they both died. One man had a knife and the other a gun. The man with the knife had been skilled, perhaps a fencer, and his knife was longer than usual, like a sword.

Karan had the impression of some events in the 1930s, or early 1940s. There had been bootlegging, with a bar open on the ground floor, and in the upper floors there was some kind of gambling establishment. She sensed many richly dressed people who went upstairs to gamble. They were more upper class than the people drinking on the first floor. There was a lot of frustration, as some men lost their rent money. There is a brass plaque on the front of the building describing the old saloon. While we were standing there, I stood in front of it so Karan could not read it.

It is interesting how closely Karan's observations matched the brass plaque. You can go and check for yourself. She told me, "Jeff, I want to go in…. now!" We did not go in, but for the future, we'll see what happens.

The Cabaret Lounge

The Caribou Club is now the Cabaret on 5th and Burnside. Randy was the manager at the Caribou from 1991 to 1994. Two sets of stairs led to the basement, which in turn led into the tunnels under the sidewalks. In the past, Burnside was hillier, and the city leveled the street by filling in the low ground. Randy had wandered through the tunnels adjoining the Caribou, and found places where ground floor storefronts became basements when the street levels were raised.

Randy sometimes heard what sounded like a party in the basement. Whenever he investigated, he found the place empty. He thought there was someone in the tunnels, but the noises did not stop, even after the tunnels were abandoned. In the 1990s, the City of Portland closed off all of the tunnel access at the street level to stop the transients from moving in. They did not want to trap any homeless people in the tunnels, so Randy and a policeman walked through the tunnels, starting at a different location, coming out near the Caribou.

They entered through an acupuncture clinic that had not one, but two basement levels. They went down one flight of stairs from street level to the basement, where they found a second flight of stairs that took them even further underground. As they walked down that tunnel, they passed from room to underground room. Most of them had some kind of furniture, discarded junk, and boxes inside. They walked into one room, and found an old bar, made of scrap wood. There was also a pool table, made of wood, which had no felt, which looked like it had never had a felt cover. Randy thought it dated to Prohibition, or perhaps was a lower class bar. They found several narrow cots, which he speculated were used by opium smokers.

As Randy and the policeman continued through the tunnels, they had heard voices or movement in the rooms ahead of them. Each time they went into a room, the voices stopped talking, but continued further on. It was becoming scary. Their flashlights could only light small portions of the rooms, leaving the rest in darkness. They did not know what was waiting out of sight. The policeman drew his pistol. They finally ran through the tunnels, chasing the voices that seemed to always stay just in front, until they found the stairs leading up to the Caribou.

Back at the Caribou, Randy never seemed able to keep one of the doors leading to the basement closed. He would find the basement door open, and so would close it, lock it, and walk away. When he came back to check on it a few minutes later, it would be unlocked and open again. On three separate occasions, the security guards believed there was someone hiding in the basement.

They had Randy stand at one entrance, near the bar. The security men started down the stairs at the other end of the building, intending to flush the intruders toward Randy. Each time, they claimed to have seen someone running away from them. They followed, only to exit the basement, and come face to face with Randy, but no intruders. Even after they checked the basement again, they could not find anyone.

The Caribou was spooky late at night, when the place was closed and quiet. Randy often heard people walking around on the second floor, above the bar and dining room. He also heard doors opening, then closing, and sounds you might expect if people lived on the upper floors. In the past, the floors above were used as a cheap hotel with small crib rooms, with a bathroom down the hall. However, the second through fourth floors above the Caribou were condemned and sealed off when Randy worked there.

One evening there was a water leak on the first floor ceiling. When he went to the second floor to investigate, Randy found water coming out of one of the second floor bathroom showers. He was puzzled. To start the water flowing on the second floor, someone had to go to his restaurant, and turn on the water main leading to the second floor, then go up to the second floor to turn the shower on. Of course, when Randy asked around, no one admitted to playing any kind of prank.

The Caribou eventually became the Cabaret, an exotic dance club, and Randy became manager at the nearby Cobalt Lounge, which became Dixie's Tavern. Unluckily for him, the spirits seemed active there too.

The Dixie Tavern

Randy was the manager of the Cobalt Lounge which is now known as the Dixie Tavern from 1994 to 1998. Before it was the Cobalt Lounge, the building was Portland's Old Town Café. On the hallway leading to the basement were pictures of people who were permanently "bounced" from the café. He estimated that there were 350 of these pictures; some of them went back to the 1950s. The owners had never removed them.

Randy marveled at the quality of the brickwork in the basement. It was one large room, which was later divided in half by a beautiful arch and wall. The first half of the basement, close to the stairs was the office, and over time, past owners had subdivided the back room, into several smaller rooms and hallways. Randy thought that these smaller rooms were linked to Portland's legendary Shanghai tunnels. He felt they could have been holding cells, where drunks waited to be sold to waiting ship's captains, although he admitted that they probably had more mundane uses. These partitions eventually became filled with boxes of junk and furniture, turning into something of a maze.

There were several tunnel entrances from other buildings into the basement. Most were not passable because they were partially blocked with phone and utility lines, or were bricked up. Despite that, the homeless managed to sneak in, and some lived in the tunnels. Randy said that more than once, the bar was empty and he had to go down to the basement, to make sure no transient had crept in. They eventually put bars on all of the windows at the Cobalt Lounge to keep out transients and robbers.

One day, Randy was in the back basement, shifting chairs and furniture. As he lit a cigarette, he turned around and saw someone walk through the large archway, and look in his direction. The figure was about ten feet away, and Randy could tell that it was a man with long hair. The man was backlit, and Randy could not see much more, but Randy thought it was a co-worker. The man turned around, and walked out, through the archway, as if he was going to the stairs. Randy called out his co-worker's name, "Frank!" but there was no response. Randy followed him, and found the outer room was empty. He did not believe that the man could have gotten up the stairs so quickly. Randy hurried up the stairs, calling for Frank. When Randy got to the ground floor, he found that the Cobalt Lounge was empty.

Randy and others heard people talking in the basement several different times. The voices were distinct, but for some reason, he could never tell what they were saying. Most of the time the voices were male. Randy thought they could have been people talking outside and the sound filtered into the basement. If so, then there should have been more female voices. Other people reported hearing someone singing, but they could not quite make out the tune. When working in the office at night, many employees heard the sound objects falling, or furniture moving in the outer room. When they investigated, some said the furniture shifted, and fell over around them. Unfortunately, they had to check out the sounds, walking very carefully.

Several times in the past, people hid in the basement, then robbed the Cobalt Lounge. Every night, the security guards searched the basement before closing. Using only flashlights, they went down the main basement stairs, through the office, into the second room, checking out the cubbies. At the far end of this second room was a single light bulb, near the stairs that led up to the kitchen. Some of the guards reported seeing shadows created by the flashlights suddenly shift and move. When they shifted the lights to shine on whoever was moving, there was no one there. Was this imagination, or was there something down there?

On the main floor, sometimes the chandelier shook, but Randy felt that this might have been the building settling. The Cobalt Lounge was a big open space, and nothing seemed to happen there, but it did on the "outer edges." A few times, as he wandered around the club, he heard patrons talking about the bathrooms. A few of them came to him, freaked out by something there. It was tantalizing, but he did not learn more. He and the rest of the staff were so busy, they did not pay too much attention to anything paranormal going on.

Before I spoke with Randy, Karan and I visited the Dixie Tavern. I did not know anything about the place, but someone had suggested it was haunted. Acting clever, I told Karan that I needed to use the restroom, and we went inside. Of course, with intuitive people, how often can you lie and get away with it? Karan and I looked around with some curiosity. Part of the décor included several pieces of lingerie, hanging from the head of a large moose head above the bar. Karan asked me, "was there was some kind of balcony, or fire escape on the wall where the bar was?"

I replied that I did not know, and though we did not see any steel posts or mounts on the wall, it was possible. When I returned, she told me that she asked our server, who said that in the past, a catwalk for go-go dancers was mounted on the wall in question. When I interviewed Randy, he confirmed that there had been a catwalk. Smiling in intuitive triumph, Karan went to use the Ladies' Room.

When she returned, she told me that she felt a female presence near the bathroom, associated with an alley nearby. When we left, we walked around the block, looking for an alley but did not see any. When I spoke with Randy, I asked him about any alleys. He told me that the go-go dancers were a bit afraid of walking to the Green Room, their break room alone. It was located down a hallway, at the end of the building, near the bathrooms. The Green Room had another door that opened up on a small outside atrium, where all of the buildings did not quite came together. It was an irregular square space, abut ten by ten foot.

I asked Randy if the atrium was all that was left of an alley, blocked when older buildings were demolished, and bigger ones were built, closing up the space. He thought it might have been true. Several of the buildings facing inside the atrium had windows or light wells, which meant that at some time, they had faced the open air. He mentioned several other blocks in Portland, where new buildings sealed off alleys. They were hidden from view at ground level, and the only people who could see them were looking out windows in places like the U.S. Bancorp Tower.

Hoodoo Antiques

Mike opened Hoodoo Antiques store on 1st and Davis in 2000, after moving from a nearby locale. When Mike opened his original store, he did not have a name for it, and spent quite a bit of time thinking of something memorable which would draw people in.

He was watching television and he saw the Rolling Stones perform *Hoodoo Voodoo Lounge*. He had a simple sign made up, using the hoodoo critter a friend drew. Mike explained that to him, and others, hoodoo was an English slang term for Voodoo, or simple magic, or something that was unexplainable.

Mike and his wife were married there that same year. As a wedding gift, Mike's mother-in-law gave him a special gift. She had worked in downtown Portland as a vendor at Saturday Market, and had a shop in the upstairs of the Erickson's Saloon building. In the past, it had been either a crib or brothel room. One day she looked at the paneling on the wall, and saw a flash of light behind the dark paneling board. When she moved the board, an old, oval pencil drawing fell out. She took it home, and kept it there for several years. When Mike got married, she had a feeling that she should give him the picture.

It was like returning something from old-town back home. He thanked her for it, and put it up above the entrance of the shop for good luck. A few weeks later, two men came into Hoodoo antiques. One of the men asked Mike if he worked in the shop at night. Mike said no. He usually closed at 6 pm, after setting motion sensor alarms. They said that was interesting, because they had walked by the shop around 3:30 am, and saw a woman, wearing a lace hat, standing in the back part of the store. Mike did not know why, but he pointed at the picture hanging above the front door. He asked if the woman in the picture was the same one they had seen. They both went a little pale and said that this was the woman.

Mike said strange incidents continued to happen. Things moved around in the shop on their own. He pointed to a teapot sitting on a table and said, "that teapot, that teapot has been here for six months. And yet, three months ago, I came in here, and could not find it to save my life. I thought

somebody had stolen it. Then two weeks went by, the teapot was back on the table. Where did it go?"

He thought of many explanations for what could have caused the disappearance. They ranged from someone moving the pot, him just missing seeing it, etc. That did not explain how it had reappeared though. Another memorable thing was a regular disturbance on New Year's Eve.

On New Year's Eve 2001, Mike received a call from his burglar alarm company, informing him that the alarms had gone off. When Mike investigated, there was no sign of entry, and nothing was touched. This happened again on New Year's Eve 2002, and in 2003. It did not happen right at midnight, but was from 10 to 30 minutes after the beginning of the New Year. After that, Mike was reluctant to go downtown to check the store on this anniversary event. But he did check, and always found that everything was in order. The exception to this was on the New Years Eve, 2006. He would have been safe celebrating with champagne, because the alarms in the antique shop were silent.

Mike said that since he had moved to the new shop, and put up the picture, he had been lucky finding the right antiques for the right people, when other antique owners had a hard time. He felt that perhaps there was some kind of Hoodoo in the mix, which brought him luck; and he did not want to risk losing it. His mother-in-law believed that a traveler had stopped at Erickson's Saloon, carrying a drawing of his beloved in an oval frame with him.

The woman who posed for the picture had really loved her man, and put something of herself into the picture. He must have been robbed, or shanghaied, and lost it. Whoever stole it sold the frame, but hid the picture instead of throwing it away. The part of the woman inside the picture looked for him even after death, and Mike's mother-in-law's impulse to give the picture to him, to take back downtown was part of that.

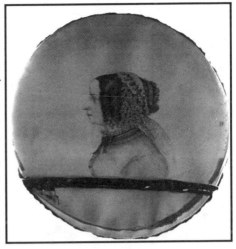

Mike will never sell his print. People expect to see it now, and he wants to keep his lucky hoodoo going. Mike also knew about possible ghosts in the Oregon Leather Company next door.

Oregon Leather Company

One day, Mike spoke with a friend named Bob, who had retired from the Oregon Leather Co. Bob was a kind of cowboy, and did not seem to be the type to believe in ghosts, or to be scared by them. Mike told the story of his haunted antique shop with Bob, and expected Bob to laugh or make fun of it. Instead, Bob shared his own story with Mike.

The store closed on Sundays, to do stocking and such. Bob said that the building used to be a brewery, and had a large basement, where they kept the beer kegs. One Sunday, Bob and another employee were in the basement, building some shelves to store merchandise. They were busy nailing the shelves together when the other man stopped. The sudden silence bothered Bob, and he looked for his partner. The man was behind Bob, pointing at the far end of the room. Bob looked down the aisles, and saw a dark, seven-foot-tall

"thing" moving along the shelves. The two of them ran out of the basement, and did not go back down for two months.

Bob and Mike went into the basement, where Mike saw a huge door, which used to open to the tunnels under the sidewalk. Workers used to take barrels of beer either to ships on the Willamette, or to a downtown bar. The door was large, and heavy because it was insulated. To protect their stock from people working in the tunnels, the brewers had riveted a set of brackets on either side of the door, and placed an iron bar across them. Simple but effective.

Bob told Mike that sometime in the past, the tunnel had been backfilled. When it was open, he could only go a few feet into the tunnels before encountering rubble and brick, which filled the tunnel from floor to ceiling. All of this seemed to be ordinary, except for the condition of the door. Bob explained to Mike that the employees always kept it locked. Or tried too. When Mike first saw it, the door was open, and the bar was on the floor several feet away. Bob told Mike that it took one or two people to hold the warped door closed, as two more people lifted the bar in the brackets. It took just as many people to move the bar away. Even so, he frequently found the bar off the brackets, and the door open, and no one admitted to opening it.

Bob gave Mike some old posters and other antiques like a lace-puller, to sell at Hoodoo Antiques. Mike took the items, but his wife made him return them, because she feared something might have "rubbed off" on them. Mike expected Bob to be puzzled, but he said, "I understand."

Old Town Pizza

Old Town Pizza is located in the ground floor of the Merchant Hotel, which took up most of the block of 2nd and Davis. Architect Warren H. Williams, who designed homes for Portland's rich and famous, drew up the plans for the Merchant Hotel. He meant for the Merchant Hotel to be a step above the nearby crib-type hotels. It was one of Portland's earliest hotels to boast its own elevator. The Merchant was built in stages between 1880 and 1884, which has led to much speculation about hidden rooms, Shanghai tunnels, and confusion about the location of certain events.

In the early 1900s, the neighborhood deteriorated, as the nearby Erickson's Hotel and surrounding Blazing Center attracted men looking for alcohol, gambling, and prostitutes.

There are rumors that even the Merchant Hotel began dealing discretely with the popular vices of the day. According to one legend, one of the prostitutes who worked at or out of the Merchant Hotel was known as Nina. Missionaries or the police convinced Nina to inform against the pimps who ran the vice houses in the area. When the pimps found out Nina had informed on them, they threw her down an elevator shaft.

Old Town Pizza operates in what used to be the lobby of the old hotel. Over the years, owners removed some of the lathe and plaster walls, and added the pizza ovens, as well as an upper dining deck. They left some fixtures from the original construction, such as the original brickwork, and tall windows. This has led to questions about events that led to the place being haunted.

One Old Town Pizza booth is in a brick room, where someone scrawled the name, Nina on one of the bricks. Some believe this is the old elevator shaft where poor Nina met her end. Since the Merchant Hotel was built in stages, it is hard to tell if this booth was an old elevator shaft, or an outside porch that was enclosed later. There is an old elevator in the upper floors but it is not in line with the booth at Old Town Pizza. However, that does not mean that Nina did not exist.

While researching my *Haunted Tour Guide*, I visited Old Town Pizza with my clairvoyant friend, Karan, who found us a table in the upstairs loft. Neither of us had heard any ghostly stories about Old Town Pizza. When I ordered a pizza, I asked the server there if the place was haunted. My memory of his reply is a bit fuzzy, but it was something like, "No, and the owners don't like us to talk about it."

Of course, if the place was not haunted, why would the owners care one way or another if the workers talked about it? At that time, there were no handouts mentioning Nina. Karan told me she sensed a presence in the loft with us. She said that it was a woman, who was oriental, or partly oriental, who had started as a simple prostitute, but gradually became a madam. She ran a brothel on the upper floors of the building. When she was alive, the madam stood where she could watch  anyone coming or going out of the building. She did that now, even after the front desk had turned into a pizza parlor.

The woman was so fixated on her position in life, that she could not perceive the fact that she was dead. Karan also said that there had been an elevator in the building, and that someone had fallen down the elevator shaft, or the elevator itself had somehow fallen to the basement. I tried communicating with the owners, who never returned my emails or phone calls.

In 2007, David Schargel and I ate at the Old Town Pizza, discussing Portland's ghosts, including the legend of Nina. He pointed out a cardholder on our table, with the Nina story in it. I skimmed over it, comparing it to Karan's impressions. David did not know who wrote the card, but seemed impressed when I told him that it had not been posted when I visited Old Town Pizza the first time. Is it possible that both Karan and the composer had gotten similar stories or impressions independently?

A 1930s ghostly experience

In the decades following the Merchant Hotel's decline from upscale clientele to hidden prostitution, there were other changes. In the second decade of the 20th century, the Merchant Hotel was important to Portland's growing Japanese population. Many families rented rooms in the hotel, and professionals such as doctors or dentists opened offices there. Unfortunately, as part of the paranoia which gripped the United States after Pearl Harbor, Japan Town, or Nihonmachi was disbanded, as the people were sent to internment camps. In 2007, I spoke with Fran S., who lived in the Merchant Hotel in the 1930s.

Fran's father had either been born in the United States, or lived there for some time. His wife came from Japan, in an arranged marriage, and they had three children. Fran, her brother and sister went to a nearby Catholic school before World War II began. Fran's family along with the rest of the Japanese-Americans were rounded up and sent to internment camps during the war. After World War II ended, some returned, but most went elsewhere. Fran eventually moved to California, and did not return to Portland for several decades.

Recently she started looking for her history on the Internet, and came across the website for Old Town Pizza. Along with pleasant childhood memories, Fran read about a ghost in the Old Town Pizza, which sounded like a less pleasant childhood memory of something that happened to her when she was around three years old, in the mid 1930s. She visited in 2007, and we looked for her old rooms.

I walked with Fran, as she tried to find her old apartment. It was not easy, after all the changes in the building. She remembered running upstairs, to their two-room apartment on the second floor, on one corner of the building. The second floor was paneled with waist high wainscoting, decorative trim, and lined with many doors. Her family apartment had one room, which served as a combination living room, kitchen, and dining room. The second room was a bedroom she shared with her parents, sister, and brother. She remembered sometimes it was so cold, her father used to block up the transom window, above the door. When we reached the second floor hallway, Fran thought that this might have been the spot where she lived.

The paint was the same shade she remembered, and the doors had transom windows over them. However, we passed the elevator, which had been "parked" on the second floor as a display. Fran did not remember an elevator near her apartment. She apologized for not remembering more details. I was amazed, I know I would not be able to remember the details of the house I lived in when I was five years old; 70 years later. We walked down a winding hallway, coming to another corner apartment. We went inside. This particular room might have been their apartment, but we will never know for sure. I believe that this room was on the second floor, above the Old Town Pizza, and the old lobby.

Fran's family were asleep when she woke up, and saw a woman walk past her, across the room. When the stranger moved, it did not seem like she walked, it was as if she was floating, in slow motion. She wore a long, dark dress. In the dark it was hard for Fran to tell what color dress the woman was wearing. It could have been black, but more likely it was a very dark gray. Fran saw mostly her back. The woman went to a dresser, and opened the top drawer. Fran saw her root around for some time, and seemingly take something out. When she closed the drawer and turned around, the woman saw that Fran was awake and watching her.

Before the woman turned around, Fran thought it was her mother. However, Fran looked at her parent's bed and saw her mother was still asleep. Fran wondered if the woman could have come in through the transom window, above the door. That did not seem likely, because her father blocked the transom off, to keep any cold air draft out.

Fran could not tell how tall the woman was, but she was probably as tall as her mother. The woman appeared to be forty, but could have been younger, because she had obviously lived a hard life. It just showed in her skin, which was wrinkled, and rough. Fran noticed that the woman was a

Caucasian, not Asian, and that she seemed surrounded by some kind of gray aura. To Fran, most people seem surrounded by a bright light, but not this woman. Fran thought, "this must be a witch."

After what was probably a long one-second pause, as they looked at each other, the woman then walked or glided out of the room. Fran did not hear the door open or close, but the woman was gone. The next day Fran told her mother about the visit. Fran's mother had kept their money and other valuables in the top drawer, but nothing was missing. Her mother told Fran that it was all a bad dream, and to forget about it. Oddly, Fran could not forget it, and remembered it again in detail over 70 years later on her return.

Fran asked me what I thought of this incident. Was this Nina, and why was she wandering the halls of the Merchant Hotel? According to my clairvoyant friend Karan, the woman who haunted the Merchant Hotel building was a self-aware spirit. She knew time had passed, and adjusted to changes in the building. She was fixated with controlling people, by spying on them. This would account for why the woman spent so much time in the upper loft of the Old Town Pizza, so she could watch the patrons. In the case of Fran and

her family, this same spirit might have been curious about her family, their doings, and financial situation. Perhaps this room had been hers in the past, or the ghost searched many of the rooms at night, when everyone was supposed to be asleep.

Portland Walking Tours begins many of their tours at Old Town Pizza, and they take many recreational ghost hunters into the basement below, showing them many of the tools of modern ghost hunting. One of the experiments they perform is trying to take spirit photos, in search of Nina. Many have captured pictures of orbs, which skeptics claim are merely dust. Or are they?

Powell's World of Books

Walter Powell, the founder of one of the best bookstores in the world, is supposed to remain somewhere in his old domain, perhaps he does not want to leave his beloved books. Some people think that he stays close to his office, and the couch,  which grew older with him. Mr. Powell used to nap on it, if he stayed too late at work, along with several other couches placed in the bookstore for customers to sit on. Despite remodels over the last decades, Mr. Powell was not confined to any particular place in the bookstore, and was reported in the Rose Room. Some people claim to have seen him near the drinking fountain. I spoke with some employees, and most of the couches and comfy chairs have been removed, and with them, perhaps Mr. Powell. Unless he hangs out at the book sculpture near the northwest entrance/exit. According to one patron, Mr. Powell's ashes were mixed in with the concrete.

Outside of Downtown Portland Proper

The noisy ghosts of Piggot's Castle

Charles Piggott's Castle in the hills southwest of Portland is a landmark to many. When seen from downtown, it seems larger than it really is. Its white painted brick towers and crenellated roofline stand out amidst the trees growing on the hillside. It was constructed in the early 1900s by Charles Piggott, a Portland lumberman and brickyard owner. He made sure that his house's four storey turreted tower overlooked what was then downtown Portland. Or did he want all of Portland to look over his new house? Like many of the Pacific Northwest's successful rich, Piggott wanted to build a showplace to illustrate the prestige of the Northwest.

He was practical enough to use bricks fired in his own business rather than imported stone. The house was a model of modern convenience, including a new-fangled speaking tube running throughout the house. It was much more efficient than the bells on ropes used in houses with fewer stories. He only lived in his castle for a year when he lost it to the bank that held the mortgage.

The evicted Piggott swore that the house would be haunted by spirits until his return. Some passersby told stories about weird noises heard coming from inside the house after Piggott died. Others told rumors of seeing shadowy figures at the windows as well. Despite this, later owners denied any strangeness.

Author Steward Holbrook came up with a possible explanation for the haunting. The house was purchased in the early 1950s, after sitting vacant for several years. The new owner removed the speaking tube system. According to Holbrook, the tubes had been picking up sounds from a train station four miles away as well as equipment and generators from a now defunct lumber mill. These sounds entered the house through the tube system's outside pickups, amplified and finally exited the tube system inside the house.

In 1971, Jack Lichtgarn purchased the house for $55,000. This was a small percentage of what it cost Piggott to have the house built several decades earlier. At that time, he had plans to renovate the house. Although Lichtgarn denied any stories of ghosts, he impressed members of the Portland Historical Landmarks Commission with stories of locked doors, secret passages and hidden sub-basements. This figured into his new plans for Piggott's Castle. He wanted to open up the house as a combination museum and restaurant, with guided mystery tours of the house. This may have perpetuated stories of the place being haunted.

Lichtgarn's plans did not last long. The Castle was sold to a family in 1979, who were still living there in 1996 when reporters for the Oregonian interviewed them. They denied having any sightings or sounds from ghosts. I visited the house on two occasions in 1998. On each occasion there was no one home to discuss the house with. Unlike many of the places mentioned in this book I would recommend against any would-be ghost hunters visiting. For one thing, the road leading to the house is very narrow and there is no parking. Another reason is the privacy of the present owners. I was not able to contact them but in their newspaper interview, they did not seem to want to talk about the house.

KWJJ is on the air

The Theodore Wilcox Mansion was built between Washington Park, and PGE Park in 1893. The first two floors of the Wilcox Mansion are constructed of sandstone and the front entryway has gilded wallpaper. There are nine marble fireplaces throughout the building. Wilcox's family lived there for several years, before moving to other locations. During World War II, a Soviet Trade Mission used the building, and after the war Ariel Rubstein, a Russian émigré, opened a music school there. He left three pianos behind when he shut down his school, and they remained until the 1990s. Radio Station KWJJ purchased the mansion in 1959. In in the 1990s, they came under new management, who oversaw upgrades in their equipment at a new building.

It is famous as one of Portland's oldest haunted landmarks. At least it was when radio station KWJJ operated there. KWJJ moved to a new location in 1997, and since then, any news of hauntings at the Wilcox Mansion have come from other sources. Before the move, I asked to investigate, and was informed that a story had already been researched. My guess would be that after Arthur Meyer's story on the radio station they became flooded with calls and visits from the curious. Myers full article is found in his book: *Ghosthunter's Guide to Haunted Landmarks, Parks, Churches, and Other Public Places.* Even after the move, I am sure ghost hunters still call or email KWJJ.

In those years, there was a lot of time to accumulate ghosts. One person saw the ghost of a woman in a black dress uniform and white hat. People thought she was a servant woman from the 1920s. Another person who had more than one experience with the ghosts in the building was disc jockey Rick Taylor. One evening Taylor was working in his sound booth when he saw a man in a white suit, and a white hat, walk to one of the large pianos. The man circled the piano, looking intently at it. Taylor saw the man again, still circling the piano. On a third occasion he was alone in the building when he heard the grand piano on the ground floor playing. Taylor was not even granted peace in the bathroom.

One evening he was using one of the bathroom stalls when he felt a strong cold breeze. He went to a bathroom cabinet to see if there was a hole or draft coming from the cabinet. He found it full of paper items. He went and sat down in the stall again. When he sat down he watched all four cabinet doors shut on their own.

When Taylor left KWJJ for a rival radio station, his replacement on the night shift met another ghostly apparition. Several times, he would see or walk by an elderly man dressed in dark trousers and a green shirt. Several more station employees have seen or heard him walking around the building from the ground floor to the attic. They feel that the ghost is that of Theodore Wilcox. No one seems to know whether this was Wilcox senior or Wilcox junior. Myers believes that it is the ghost of Wilcox junior, who would be more inclined to dress casually than his straight-laced businessman father. He believes the man in white to be one of the many musicians who taught there, when the building was a music school.

Pittock Mansion

Historic Pittock Mansion, the 16,000 square foot building that overlooks Portland is one of Portland's grandest homes. Local craftsmen built it almost entirely of regional materials. Architect Edward T. Foulkes' designed a square building, with circular rooms off a central staircase like spokes from a wheel. The house had many modern features, including a dumbwaiter to raise food to the upstairs bedrooms. The morning airflow acted to cool the house without fans in the summer. Instead of bells to call servants, the Pittocks had an internal phone system installed. A central vacuum system ran throughout the house. According to stories, the vacuum was so powerful that if it was used when the windows were closed, the windows would implode.

Georgiana Pittock saved the silver foil that her tea had come wrapped in. When the house was built, she used the foil to paper the vaulted ceiling of the entryway of the house.

The Pittocks stood apart from their peers, in a time when the rising upper classes of the Pacific Northwest were "visionary-despots." While some of them did things that might be criminal today, without their dedication, work, and yes, their vision of progress, we would not have the benefits we enjoy today. At the same time, the men and women who undertook the development of the Pacific Northwest could be short sighted and ruthless in accomplishing their goals. The Pittock's ideals of public service set the Pittocks apart.

Georgiana Pittock helped found the Ladies' Relief Society in 1867. This included a Children's Home, which provided support for Portland's needy children. Working with the Woman's Union, she helped establish the Martha Washington Home for single working women. Her love of flowers was the genesis of Portland's Rose Festival. Henry Pittock helped found the Mazamas climbing club and was part of the first expedition to climb Mt. Hood. He frequently led the Rose Parade, which started at the mansion.

The house was not completed until they had been married 58 years. After the sandstone mansion was completed, the Pittocks and some of their descendents moved in together. Georgiana lived in the house for four years, until her death in 1918. Henry survived her by one year and died in 1919. The house was purchased by the City of Portland in 1964 and restored with public and donated funds and labor.

Since the house opened to the public in 1965, stories of strange happenings grew. A picture of Henry Pittock as a young man seems to move from place to place. It usually hangs on a bedroom mantle, but will move to different locations only minutes after it was last seen. Visitors have come forward with their own stories. Some have reported the strong smell of roses, when there were none in the house. This was Georgiana's favorite flower. Other people have reported the sound of heavy boots walking in or out of the rear entrance. A woman was looking at the picture displays in the basement level when she felt something. She turned around and saw the figure of an elderly woman, standing next to her. The woman vanished, before her eyes.

A group of native Hawaiians had taken the tour and as they left one of the youths remarked; "My uncle is a shaman in Hawaii and he says that he can feel the spirits of the Pittocks here, and they are very happy."

One guide said that one morning she entered the mansion and saw a figure standing in one of the ground floor rooms as she turned on the lights...only to find it was a new mannequin display. Perhaps that is why they are hesitant to talk about their own experiences. When I visited the mansion in the summer of 1998, I took a chance and asked one of the museum staff if the ghosts were acting up lately.

I was told, "It's strange that you asked. One of the windows overlooking the front entrance shut and latched on its own earlier this morning."

When I took the tour I examined the window. It is situated on the first landing of the staircase on the main hall. The heavy glass pane could have blown closed on its own, but not likely. The latch is the kind that takes a human hand to lift and turn to close. I do not see how it could have latched on its own. It was a hot summer day. Perhaps someone besides the staff felt that the air coming in was too warm and decided to close the window. Perhaps not.

The Willamette and East Portland

The Steel Bridge

The first railroad bridge across the Willamette River was built in 1888. Because they used steel rather than iron to build it, people called it the Steel Bridge. In 1912, the Union Pacific and Oregon Railway and Navigation Company replaced it with the current bridge, which Portlanders called the Steel Bridge as well. The current Steel Bridge is a truss bridge with lifting decks. What that means is the trusses that support the bridge are located on its outer edges, and traffic crosses on the inside, and it has two decks for traffic, which can lift up to allow tall ships to sail underneath.

Cars and MAX light rail use the upper deck, while the lower deck has separate paths for full size trains, and pedestrians. Both decks can lift independently, making it the only one of its kind in the world. The lower deck is 26 feet above the normal river level, and the upper deck is 72 above it. The lower deck can raise those 72 feet in about 20 seconds. When this happens, pedestrians should not try to run across the bridge, since the lower span fits VERY tightly into the upper. When both spans are raised, they go up to 163 feet above the Willamette River. Unfortunately, the Steel Bridge, like other Portland bridges has been favored by suicides.

People who commit suicide usually fall into two categories. They are people who have a terrible pain they cannot deal with, or they are angry, and want to make some kind of statement. Some suicides are both. Some people make suicide pacts, these are mostly elderly couples, one of whom is dying, and their partner, who cannot live without the other. A number of teenage couples also try, usually unsuccessfully to kill themselves. On July 2nd, 1998, a couple who did not quite fit any pattern succeeded with tragic results.

On that sunny afternoon, several people saw a couple wearing a mix of heavy shirts, shorts, and leather boots walking across the top span of the Steel Bridge. The man, aged 29, and the woman, aged 25, may have looked a bit too old to be Goths or Skinheads. No one saw them pause and take out ropes with a noose on each end, and fasten them to the bridge; and put the nooses around their necks. One man in an office saw them jump off the bridge, but thought they were mannequins, as part of a publicity stunt.

He was wrong. Within a few minutes, the police stopped traffic from crossing the upper span of the Steel Bridge. They could not remove the bodies immediately. While they were investigating, the police could not stop the departure of an AMTRAK train, on the lower deck. Although the authorities on the train warned people to keep their windows rolled up, and not look out, many did, perhaps while the police were lowering the bodies to a boat floating on the Willamette River, below.

The man, Michael, wore a backpack around his chest, and the police found a 13 page suicide note inside. He wrote that he was a heroin addict and had sold all he had to support his habit. Life was too hard for him to go on. Sadly, his girlfriend Mora had apparently tried to talk him out of his suicide, but had lost hope herself. No one has reported seeing them reliving their tragic fall. Fortunately.

The White Eagle Saloon

One of Portland's most famous haunts is the White Eagle Saloon, located in what was the town of Albina. In the mid 1800s, the east bank of the Willamette River had a hodge-podge of house boats and cabins built along the lower shores of the river. Gradually a series of planned towns arose.

In 1872, Edwin Russell, William Page, and George Williams laid out a town they called Albina, which was the first name of Page's wife. They sited their little town around a new ferry landing, and the little town grew quickly. Especially when train lines went in nearby.

Most of the people who settled there were Germans, Russians, and many Poles. As Albina grew, its core was surrounded by Alberta on the north, NE 15th on the east, NE Russell on the south, and NE Albina on the west. Russell Street had a reputation for being the tough part of Albina. Thirty saloons lined Russell Street, from the ferry slip, east to what is now Martin Luther King Way. The ferry continued to run between east west Portland until 1929. Eventually, the city of Portland annexed Albina. A survivor of those early days was the White Eagle Saloon.

The White Eagle's history

The McMenamins bought the White Eagle in the 1990s, and their historian has done research confirming some of the myths surrounding the White Eagle, and proving the others false. Of course, other sources do not agree with this research.

According to Chuck Hughes, who owned the White Eagle in the 1980s and 1990s, there has been an eating and drinking establishment on the site of the White Eagle since the 1850s. This seems unlikely, since Albina was not laid out until the 1870s. According to Hughes, the original saloon was built of wood. Building lots were so small, buildings were built touching each other, with no alleys or fences between neighbors. There was a picture hanging at the White Eagle that showed Russell Street's crowded conditions.

There might have been a smaller bar built on the site before the present White Eagle, even if it was not as early as the 1850s. The White Eagle's entryway has a Navaho pattern tile floor laid over a concrete slab, which runs about half the length of the White Eagle. The rest of the White Eagle floor is made of wood joists and sub flooring. The cast cement that makes up the walls of the basement are definitely two different ages. One set of concrete is the same length as the slab above, and the second pouring follows the present floor plan. This suggests that a smaller building stood on the same site before the current building was built, and they enlarged the basement for the new one.

The present brick bar and café was built between 1905 and 1906. Surviving Liquor Board records for the White Eagle go back to 1906. It was known as the *B. Soboleski & Company Saloon*, owned by a Barney Soboleski and William Hryszko, and their bartender was Joseph Hryszko. In 1909, at least one of the Hryszko's roomed at 118 ½ Russell, which was the top floor of the White Eagle. Barney Soboleski was on the rolls until 1914, when the Hryszko brothers apparently became sole owners.

One of the historic questions about the White Eagle is, "when they started letting out the rooms on the second floor?" The answer is, "probably as soon as it was built."

The White Eagle has a separate entrance and staircase to the right of the main entrance. It is original construction, not an add on. At that time, people often built brick shells, and finished them when they had funding. How long it took to finish the second floor is an open question. The Hryszkos lived on the upper floor by at least 1909. The report shows that Bruno and Bronislaw Soboleski either worked there, or lived in the upper story, in 1914, which suggests that the second floor was finished, and open for rent by that time.

A few years later, in 1917, the tax rolls change the use of the building from a saloon, to selling soft drinks. This is probably due to the beginnings of Prohibition. Even before Congress ratified the 18th Amendment in 1919, many states like Oregon had passed their own anti-alcohol laws. In 1931, Portland began the Great Renumbering, and the White Eagle got its present street number of 836 North Russell, in 1933.

That same year, with the repeal of Prohibition, it proudly became a beer parlor and restaurant. Under continued Hryszko ownership, the saloon changed names several times, becoming the White Eagle Café in 1949. In 1956, the name Hryszko changed its spelling into Riscoe, and the family continued ownership for many more years.

One of the managers in the 1970s was Tony Ferrena, who may have been related to the Riscoes. He made the place famous as a rock music venue, hosting local bands such as the Rascoes and the Holy Moddle Rounders. Some of his hand drawn posters still hang in the White Eagle. Chuck Hughes purchased or rented the White Eagle in 1979, and he owned it until selling to the McMenamins Brothers in the late 1990s.

Fixtures at the White Eagle

Visitors to the White Eagle may admire the bar. It is a huge ornate oak affair with columns bracketing a large mirror. According to Chuck Hughes, the bar came around the Horn, as the tip of South America was known, decades earlier. It shows up in several old pictures of the White Eagle. These photos show that the position of the bar has changed. Today, the bar is located about halfway down the building, but in the past, it was near the front entrance, bordered by the tile floor. When Chuck Hughes bought the White Eagle, he had to move the bar, and section off a portion of the building to seat minors. When

Hughes moved the bar, he hid an interesting historic feature.

Some historians discuss the difference between a bar, a tavern, and a saloon. A bar was a place where men and women could drink together. Depending on state laws, women might have to be escorted by a man, or they could not stand at the bar, but had to sit at a table. A tavern was a place where men and women could go, and there was some kind of food served as well. There might even be a room or two available for overnight guests. A saloon was definitely a place where men were the only customers allowed. The exception to this might be waitresses, or saloon gals.

Because the White Eagle was a saloon, women were not allowed inside. The owners built an open urinal at the base of the bar. Customers had only to open their pants to relieve themselves, to avoid leaving a drink, or losing a spot at the bar. There was a system of water pipes to flush the urine out of the building. Some of the historic photographs of the White Eagle show the urinal, even after the place was open as a sandwich shop during Prohibition. Though I am sure that by that time, customers used the approved restroom. An examination of the current bar showed that someone had filled in the urinal, and then covered it up with mats.

The White Eagle's darker history

The construction and ownership of the White Eagle is fairly well documented. The controversy comes from stories that the White Eagle was a den of prostitution as well as a working man's bar. In these legends, the second storey of the bar was used as a combination bordello and boarding house. The prostitutes allowed in the upper floors were white, while oriental or black prostitutes were confined to the basement. This operation was run by an oriental bouncer, who kept order in the second floor of the bar, as well as the basement. Again, as in many other Portland drinking establishments, there were rumors of Shanghai tunnels in the basement.

When the McMenamins purchased the White Eagle, their historian interviewed one of the Riscoes. The man told Hills that his parents would have never allowed prostitutes inside their building, much less maintained a brothel. How does this compare with the legends?

It seems likely that the real history is somewhere in between. I have seen the basement, where the colored prostitutes were supposedly kept, where opium was sold, and sailors were shanghaied. There was a coal chute and freight opening into the sidewalk above. There was no sign of a vast Shanghai tunnel network. On the other hand, there were a few light wells in the sidewalk to the west, suggesting that a long time ago there might have been some kind of tunnel running from building to building. In the late 19th century, the waterfront was just to the west of Interstate Avenue.

When looking back at the historic nature of the Albina neighborhood it is likely that some of the White Eagle's customers had dealings with prostitutes. At that time, these men worked hard, drank hard, and lived hard. While they probably did not operate a brothel, if the owners of the White Eagle had not turned a blind eye, or at least winked when one of their customers wanted a room for himself and a girl, their patrons would have drank somewhere else. The same thing goes for drinking during Prohibition.

The history of White Eagle employee Sam Worek is also hard to separate from the myth. According to one legend, Sam Worek was abandoned near the tavern when he was a child. He had a cleft palette and may have been mildly mentally retarded. Sam was more or less adopted by the Hryszko family, and worked at the saloon, helping where he could in return for room, board and a small salary. In the 1950s, the Riscoes were closing off the upper floor, and Sam was worried about finding a place to live. He thought he had found a place, and that night before he moved, he went to bed and died in his sleep. His possessions were left in his room.

According to others, Sam was an adult when he came to the White Eagle. He was an excellent cook, but had a weakness for the bottle. When he went on a "bender," he would disappear for days or weeks at a time. When he returned, he would go back to his kitchen, until the next time the bottle called. He was in his 60s or 70s when he died. There is a picture hanging in the White Eagle, dating to the early 1900s. It shows the Hryszko family, and an adult Sam posing for the camera. Sam is the dapper dark haired fellow with a lock of hair in his eyes staring at the camera. He appears to be in his late 20's or early 30's. According to some tax documents, Sam Worek lived in the upper storey of the White Eagle (at least) between 1950 and 1956.

One interesting thing about the rooms is a lack of closet space. Most of the rooms were built in groups of three, and each of these rooms had a window opening up into a central light well. The rooms were lower rent cribs, around 10 foot by 10 foot, with a small sink, but no built in closets. There were commodes and bathtub rooms off the central hall.

The Hryszkos probably lived in Rooms 1 and 2 in the front of the building. A common door joined these rooms, and Room 2 had a small built in closet. I guess that Room 1 was their sitting room, and Room 2 was their bedroom. The room backing onto Room 2, now numbered Room 3, also had a small closet, suggesting it was built for a long term boarder. Several people suggested this was Sam's room.

White Eagle ghost stories

It is hard to separate fact from fiction, and witness reports from urban legends when it comes to the White Eagle. Author Jessica Salmonson saw a TV spot on the White Eagle, and wrote a story where her fictional heroine visited the White Eagle, and saw a ghostly repeat of a murder there. In the story, her heroine watched a prostitute named Rose (aren't they all named Rose?) murdered by her alcoholic boyfriend Sam. Her story was published but some newspapers left off the disclaimer that it was fictional. People have posted it on the Internet with the same omission.

One of the wonderful things about haunted houses (for authors) is that as time goes by the number of ghost stories continue to grow. This is especially true of Portland's most famous haunted drinking establishment. I can only briefly summarize some of the older stories from the White Eagle here. I am afraid that to learn more, readers will have to read my earlier works.

Chuck Hughes told of many strange happenings at the White Eagle in the years he owned it. In the ladies bathroom, more than one customer would be using one of the stalls, when a piece of toilet paper would fly over from the other stall. After a fun and active toilet paper fight, the customer would prepare to leave, only to find that the other stall was empty. In the men's room, the commode would flush on its own, late at night. Chuck Hughes replaced it more than once and still had the problem. But the weirdest things happened in the basement and upper floor.

One of the employees was standing at the head of the basement stairs, when she felt something push her. The woman fell to the foot of the stairs; well half fell, half floated and landed unhurt. When she looked up, she watched a mop bucket float down the stairs toward her. Chuck Hughes used to go onto the second floor, which was condemned when he owned the White Eagle, to adjust the heating system. People claimed to have seen a woman standing in front of the window of Room 2, looking outward.

When Chuck ran up the stairs, no one was there. Many times he would find doors open. Since he was the only one to go up there, Chuck remembered closing them on his prior visit. He used to let curiosity seekers onto the second floor. One group could not get a door to open, no matter how hard they pulled on the doorknob. Oddly, after they gave up, the door opened on its own. Unfortunately, another group broke into several rooms, and stole items like (Sam's?) clothing, as well as room numbers and doorknobs.

After Chuck sold the White Eagle, it began a new incarnation, when the McMenamins renovated the upper floor and opened it to guests. Soon after the new staff began working at the White Eagle, one man was carrying supplies in the basement. He walked by the large freezer with his arms full of food. As he passed the freezer, one of the doors opened and hit him in the back. This was a large restaurant freezer with doors that automatically latched when closed. It is possible that the last person who opened the freezer did not close the door completely and it did not latch properly. It is also possible but improbable, that the vibration of his passing had caused the door to swing open as he passed.

Someone added a new fixture at the bar in 1991. It was a 12 inch mechanical bartender toy from the 1950s. It was designed to raise one arm holding a martini mixer, shake the arm, then pour the martini into a glass held in the other arm, and finally raise the glass. Although there were batteries in the toy it had not worked since it was brought to the bar. One of the bartenders, Bill was speaking to a skeptical customer about the White Eagle being haunted. Both kind of agreed there were no such things as ghosts. As soon as Bill finished talking about the ghost, the toy began to work. It no longer sits on the bar, but is kept in a cabinet behind it.

I visited the White Eagle with a female friend in January of 2000. She knew that strange things had happened in the bathroom, but was not sure what to expect. She was using the restroom when she heard a metallic snick. She thought someone had unlocked the stall door next to her. She was surprised because she could not see any feet in the stall next to her. There was no other sound. She looked around the stall and discovered that it was not the lock on the stall next door that had locked. She saw that her stall door had somehow unlocked itself.

One afternoon, Jeff was standing just inside the kitchen area, counting tips. To his right was the stairway leading down to the basement. The basement has been a focus of strange activity in the past. Some time earlier, an employee had wedged a spare menu board between the right hand wall of the doorsill and the pipes an inch or two from the wall. For some reason, Jeff turned his head and looked at the stairway. He saw the menu board fly from its place, on the right side of the doorway, across the doorway, where it struck against the left-hand wall with a loud slap.

A ghost night at the White Eagle Saloon

Several years ago, I rented the top floor of the White Eagle, and everyone who stayed there was interested in the paranormal. Many people identified a cold spot near the front of the building. It was not a breeze, but seemed centered in one area, and it did not move. Some people smelled strong floral perfume, "like your grandmother used to wear."

Since I was the one with all the room keys, my wife and I took Room 2, which fronts the street. It is also the room where people have seen the ghost Rose, looking outward. Because some people are reluctant to use Ouija boards, we had our first attempt there. I monitored an EMF detector while several people attempted to contact Sam or Rose. I noticed a curious trend recorded by the EMF detector.

Most of the time, the energy reading on the EMF detector was around 1.1 to 2.0. When they began their séance, the meter quickly went up to 5 or 6. At one point, it spiked at 7.5. I do not have any conclusions as to the significance of this, but it is very curious that when they stopped, the readings went down again. In another attempt, whenever they asked questions about Sam, the meter reading would go down. They concluded that the spirits they contacted did not want to talk about him.

The tours begin

In 2007, I met with David Schargel and members of the Portland Walking Tours at the White Eagle, where his *Beyond Bizarre* tour stops. I wanted to familiarize everyone with the basics of ghost hunting terminology and techniques. It was also a chance for them to visit one of Portland's premier haunts. We rented Rooms 1 and 2. While checking in, David spoke with the McMenamins staff. My clairvoyant friend Karan arrived around midnight to discuss an intuitive approach to paranormal investigations. She took the people on a short tour of the upstairs hallway, discussing pressure changes, and how the body is sensitive to the paranormal.

Later we entered Room 2. Karan stood at the entrance to the closet, and said that the man was in the adjoining room (Number 3) and was afraid to come into Room 2, because of Karan and myself. One of the guides sat on the bed, facing Karan and the closet. He held a Tri-field EMF meter, and said the background energy seemed steady around 7 miligaus. I asked Karan to bring the man into the room. She said she would try. While she did this, the meter levels fluctuated slightly, and the energy dropped from 7 to around 5 miligaus. Karan discussed the entity for several minutes, and suggested

he should be forced out of the room. She faced the back of the closet, and stood there for several minutes. Slowly, the baseline energy reading went back to around 7 miligaus.

This is, of course, not proof that there was a ghost there. However, as everyone stood in the room, there were no obvious reasons why the readings should have changed (coincidentally.) No one activated any electronic devices, nor did they turn any off. Everyone stood basically in the same places, and there were no other changes to the local environment. So if this was a coincidence, the meter going up and then down, it was a mighty convenient one.

The Portland Walking Tours bring some of their tours onto the second floor of the White Eagle. Armed with EMF detectors, cameras, and their senses, the tour group has an opportunity to see if they can find any evidence of the paranormal. Paranormal events do not happen on command, and many do not experience anything outrageous, but others have. One tour group found a cold spot near Room 1. They were able to walk around it, and put their hands in it from different angles. It was not a draft, and it did not move. After a few minutes, it dissipated. A different group was spread out down the hallway, when their guide noticed that their EMF detectors started lighting up, as the background energy spiked. What was unusual was how it happened.

There were three people with meters. The meter of the person closest to him spiked. A few seconds later, the person in the middle of the hallway spiked. A few seconds after that, the meter of the person at the far end of the hallway spiked. A few seconds later, the meter at the far end spiked again, then the middle, then the closest meter spiked. This pattern repeated itself two more times before it stopped. Was someone on the roof walking back and forth, carrying some kind of energy device like a phone? On the other hand, was there an invisible ghost pacing the hallway, waiting for the tourists to leave?

Index

About the Author

Jeff Davis was born in the Pacific Northwest, and has degrees in Anthropology and Archaeology. He has worked and traveled widely throughout Washington and Oregon. His background and curiosity about the paranormal helped Jeff research and write six books on paranormal events of the region. He has contributed stories to the Weird US book, *Weird Hauntings*. He is currently writing *Weird Oregon*, after finishing *Weird Washington* for Barnes and Noble.

He has appeared on the History Channel's *Haunted History* and has been heard on *Coast-to-Coast AM* and the *Lou Gentile Show*. He worked as a creative consultant for the Lincoln County and Kutz Productions for the video, *Oregon Ghost Explorer*. Jeff has also been a guest on many of the Northwest's television and radio stations. Jeff regularly makes public appearances at colleges, talking about the paranormal.

His website: *www.ghostsandcritters.com* is one of the oldest websites in the Pacific Northwest to give evidence of the paranormal in the region. Jeff lives in Vancouver, Washington with his wife and two spoiled cats. His more mundane activities include running his own small publishing business and the occasional firewalk.

Other Books By Jeff Davis

Ghosts and Strange Critters of Washington and Oregon

Ghosts, Critters and Sacred Places of Washington and Oregon

Ghosts, Critters and Sacred Places of Washington and Oregon II

Ghosts, Critters and Sacred Places of Washington and Oregon III

A Haunted Tour Guide to the Pacific Northwest

Haunted Astoria

With Al Eufrasio

Weird Washington

Weird Oregon
(in 2009)